Social Networks *and* Organizations

Martin Kilduff
Wenpin Tsai

SAGE Publications
London • Thousand Oaks • New Delhi

© Martin Kilduff Wenpin Tsai

First published 2003

Apart from any fair dealing for the purposes of research
or private study, or criticism or review, as permitted
under the Copyright, Designs and Patents Act, 1988, this
publication may be reproduced, stored or transmitted
in any form, or by any means, only with the prior
permission in writing of the publishers, or in the case of
reprographic reproduction, in accordance with the terms
of licences issued by the Copyright Licensing Agency.
Enquiries concerning reproduction outside those terms
should be sent to the publishers.

 SAGE Publications Ltd
6 Bonhill Street
London EC2A 4PU

SAGE Publications Inc
2455 Teller Road
Thousand Oaks, California 91320

SAGE Publications India Pvt Ltd
B-42, Panchsheel Enclave
Post Box 4109
New Delhi 100 017

British Library Cataloguing in Publication data

A catalogue record for this book is available
from the British Library

ISBN 0 7619 6956 X
ISBN 0 7619 6957 8 (pbk)

Library of Congress Control Number available

Typeset by C&M Digitals (P) Ltd., Chennai, India
Printed in Great Britain by Athenaeum Press, Gateshead

Contents

Acknowledgements

We thank the following for their helpful comments on previous drafts of this book: Dan Brass, Denny Gioia, Don Hambrick, Mihaela Keleman, Michael Launsbury, Ajay Mehra and Hongseok Oh.

1 Introduction

On the night of 17 April 1775, two men rode different routes from outside Boston to Lexington warning communities along the way of the imminent threat from the British army. The message delivered by Paul Revere and William Dawes on their midnight rides was dramatic: the next day would see the British army marching on Lexington to arrest colonial leaders and then on to Concord to seize colonial guns and ammunition. Both Revere and Dawes carried the identical message through just as many towns over just as many miles. Paul Revere's message spread like wildfire in communities such as Charlestown and Medford, but Dawes's message failed to catch fire, with the result that in towns such as Waltham even the local militia leaders weren't aware of the British moves. Why was there a difference in the reception of this identical message? Evidence suggests that Paul Revere was connected to an extensive network of strategic relationships whereas William Dawes's connections were less useful. Paul Revere 'knew everybody. … When he came upon a town, he would have known exactly whose door to knock on, who the local militia leader was, who the key players in town were' (Gladwell, 2000: 23). Not only did Revere alert whole towns to the looming threat, the leaders in these towns themselves sent riders to alert the surrounding areas. Dawes's message failed to spread through the network whereas Revere's message rapidly diffused.

The moral of this tale is that the network of relationships within which we are embedded may have important consequences for the success or failure of our projects. Evidence suggests that the types of network we form around ourselves affect everything from our health, to our career success, to our very identities. One study of a randomly selected sample of 6,928 residents of Alameda County, California, over a nine-year period showed that people who 'lacked social and community ties were more likely to die ... than those with more extensive contacts' (Berkman and Syme, 1979: 186). The study controlled for a host of other possible causes of mortality, such as smoking, alcohol consumption, obesity, physical activity and utilization of preventive health services. A follow-up study looked at the same sample over a 17-year period and confirmed these results, but also found that extensive contact with friends and relatives (compared to contact with spouse) was particularly important in reducing mortality for those over the age of 60 (Seeman et al., 1987). Another study showed that maintaining a diverse network reduced susceptibility to the common cold (Cohen et al., 1997). People who had frequent contact (in person or on the telephone) to others across a wide range of relationship types (relatives, neighbours, friends, workmates, members of social groups, etc.) tended to resist infection better than those whose contacts were with a narrower range of relationship types. Maintaining network ties to different groups of people in organizations has been associated with higher performance ratings (Mehra et al., 2001), and faster promotions (Burt, 1992). Having the right contacts can help you get a job (Granovetter, 1974) and can help you negotiate a higher salary (Seidel et al., 2000).

The extent to which people are engaged in social activities in the community may be important not only for the individuals concerned but also for the larger collectivity, according to one version of social capital theory. In this perspective, for any community, the higher the level of citizen engagement in civic life and in voluntary organizations such as sports clubs, the better the overall economic health of the community (e.g., Putnam, 1993). The jury is still out as to whether social capital measured at the individual level does indeed have effects at the community level (Portes, 2000). A similar argument at the organizational level also awaits testing. This argument suggests that individuals' good citizenship behaviours in organizations helps create organizational social capital that in turn positively affects firm performance (Bolino et al., 2002).

We have focused on the positive effects of network ties and social capital, but we also know that maintaining relationships with people requires resources that some groups of people find it difficult to afford (Riley and Eckenrode, 1986). Problems with relationships can adversely affect people's well-being (Rook, 1984). People in close relationships such as friendship have the opportunity to betray each other's trust and to hurt each other in other ways (Granovetter, 1985). Increasing research attention is being directed towards the negative side of social interaction (e.g., Brass and Labianca, 1999; Yager, 2002).

Social relationships affect not only people's well-being, but also their very identities. Adam Smith declared that 'the countenance and behaviour of those [we live] with … is the only looking glass by which we can, in some measure, with the eyes of other people, scrutinize the propriety of our conduct' (quoted in Bryson, 1945: 161). George Herbert Mead (1934: 171) summarized this perspective most succinctly in his remark that the individual only becomes a self 'in so far as he can take the attitude of another and act toward himself as others act'.

Despite the apparently decisive effects that social contacts can have on the lives and well-being of individuals, much social science research has been silent concerning social influences. In the area of decision-making, for example, both the normative models, such as expected utility theory (e.g., Becker, 1976), and the descriptive models, such as prospect theory (Kahneman and Tversky, 1979), portray individuals making decisions in splendid isolation from the force-field of influences that surround them. As a survey of social network analysis pointed out: 'In the atomistic perspectives typically assumed by economics and psychology, individual actors are depicted as making choices and acting without regard to the behavior of other actors' (Knoke and Kuklinski, 1982: 9). In the field of organizational behaviour, the dominance of atomistic approaches such as expectancy theory has contributed to the neglect of social influences.

The neglect of social context has affected not only the more individualistic social sciences of economics and psychology, but also the more structural approaches such as sociology (including organizational sociology). Many sociologists continue to study categories that are assumed to share similar characteristics (Wellman, 1988a: 15). These categories, such as 'managers', 'employed adults', and 'churchgoers', contain aggregated sets of unrelated individuals. Much analysis consists of investigating whether individuals in one set, such as managers, are more likely to belong to another set, such as high-performers. At the organizational level of analysis, enquiries examine whether characteristics such as size and concentration of authority predict important outcomes such as market share. These analyses tell us little about how the structure of actors' social worlds emerges, and how the structure of interactions affects outcomes.

Studies of organizational social networks have increased in recent years in response to this perceived neglect of social structure and interaction. Useful collections of articles have been published containing original research and thinking concerning social capital (Leenders and Gabbay, 1999) and network ties (Andrews and Knoke, 1999; Grandori, 1999; Nohria and Eccles, 1992). Several monographs have advanced our understanding of specialized topics such as structural holes (Burt, 1992), job-search networks (Granovetter, 1995) and inter-firm alliances (Nooteboom, 1999). Useful reviews of research have focused on networks at the intraorganizational level (Flap et al., 1998; Krackhardt and Brass, 1994; Raider and Krackhardt, 2002), the organizational level (Gulati et al., 2002) and the interorganizational level (Baker and Faulkner, 2002). The field of practitioner-oriented books includes recommendations concerning organizational architecture (e.g., Helgesen, 1995) and managerial relationship-building (e.g., Baker, 1994, 2000). And books of methods have proliferated (e.g., Degenne and Forse, 1999; Knoke and Kuklinski, 1982; Schensul et al., 1999; Scott, 2000; Wasserman and Faust, 1994).

With all of this existing literature, what is the motivation for the current book? Our intention is to provide a compact handbook that introduces major concepts, covers the rudiments of methods, explores major debates, directs attention to new theoretical directions, and presents a vigorous critique of some taken-for-granted assumptions. Our book is aimed at all of those who seek a lucid and lively treatment of social network approaches to organizational research, with a particular emphasis on the neglected area of inter-personal networks in organizations. We aspire to offer new insights to those familiar with network analysis, and to motivate those interested in pursuing network research to embark on journeys of discovery.

The potential application of the social network approach to organizations is, in our view, enormous. The full spectrum of organizational phenomena that network thinking can illuminate extends across levels from micro to macro, and includes topics typically covered in fields such as organizational cognition, organizational behaviour, organizational theory, and strategic management. Network research investigates relational processes and structures at many different levels of analysis. We organize our review of potential applications by unit of observation (the individual, the team, the organization, etc.) and within these units by level of analysis.

EXPLORING THE RANGE OF ORGANIZATIONAL SOCIAL NETWORK RESEARCH

Individual Level of Observation

Cognition
Cognitions concerning organizational networks matter. If your colleagues at work think that a prominent person in the organization is your friend, then your colleagues will tend to think of you as a high performer: the perceived friendship link to the prominent person will bathe you in reflected glory. What matters is the perception that you have the friendship tie – irrespective of whether there really is such a tie or not (Kilduff and Krackhardt, 1994). One of the most interesting areas of social network research in organizations concerns such network perceptions.

Where do these perceptions come from? Learning happens as a result of personal interactions between the individual and others: people learn who their friends are. But people also learn by observing others' interactions, by noticing, for example, who is friendly with whom among not only their own circle of friends but also among those outside of this circle. Research on network learning shows that individuals expect network relationships to follow certain patterns. For example, people expect to see friendship relations between two individuals as reciprocated rather than as an unrequited flow of friendship from one person to the other (De Soto, 1960). People tend to bias their perceptions of network relations in organizations in the direction of such expectations (Krackhardt and Kilduff, 1999).

Thus each individual develops a more or less accurate map of the relationships between all the people in an organizational department or other social arena in which the individual is routinely involved. Individual cognitive maps of a social network can differ widely from one person to another for a variety of reasons that are still not well understood but that might include factors such as susceptibility to biased perceptions, differential opportunities to learn the social network, individual position in the organization, and so on. People who are more accurate in their perceptions may gain advantages in organizations. For example, one study showed that having an accurate perception of who goes to whom for advice in an organization significantly predicted how powerful the individual was perceived to be by others (Krackhardt, 1990). In our view, there is great potential for further work from a social network perspective at the cognitive level of analysis. We spend time in Chapter 4 outlining an emerging cognitive network theory and its implications for organizational analysis.

Relations between individuals

Networks exist not only as sets of cognitions inside the heads of individuals in organizations, but also as structures of constraint and opportunity negotiated and reinforced between interacting individuals. People tend to rely on others in their networks for help in making major decisions (Kilduff, 1990). Further, employees not only tend to interact with group members who are similar on distinctive attributes such as ethnicity and gender (Ibarra, 1992), but the lower the relative proportion of such group members in the organization, the higher the likelihood of within-group identification and friendship (Mehra et al., 1998).

Given the general preference people have for social interaction with others similar to themselves, there arise opportunities for those who bridge across social divides. People whose network connections allow them to act as go-betweens in organizations, connecting otherwise disconnected individuals and groups, tend to garner many benefits, including faster promotions (Podolny and Baron, 1997). One of the newest areas of research concerns the ways in which people of different personality types tend to build distinctively different types of network connection (with respect to spanning across social divides, for example). We outline an emerging personality approach to social structure and discuss its relevance for organizational network research in Chapter 4. Potential applications of interpersonal network research include such standard organizational topics as power, job design, motivation and leadership (Krackhardt and Brass, 1994). Much of this work remains to be done.

Dyads, triads and cliques

There is unrealized potential for looking at two- and three-person units within network structures. Some recent work has taken network data collected at the individual level and used it to examine the ways in which a certain type of two-person unit (or 'dyad') experiences organizational life. The basic idea is that pairs of friends who have friends in common (compared to pairs of friends who have no friends in common) are likely to find themselves constrained in their attitudes and behaviours. For example, if Stacy and Kay have a disagreement and become angry with each other concerning some organizational decision, they are likely to repair their wounded feelings if they have mutual friends who can intercede, and whose relationships would also be disrupted by any breach between Stacy and Kay. This emerging stream of work suggests looking carefully at the network contexts in which pairs of individuals are located. (See Krackhardt, 1998, 1999; Krackhardt and Kilduff, 2002, for more on this.)

A three-person group is quite different from a two-person group in that coalitions, mediation, and a host of other sociological processes become possible (see Fernandez and Gould, 1994, for a recent treatment of this topic). Three-person groups (known as 'triads') have long been considered the building blocks of informal networks (Holland and Leinhardt, 1977) but have been relatively neglected in organizational network research (but see Krackhardt and Kilduff, 1999, for recent work).

Similarly neglected in organizational research (despite a rich tradition of research in sociology) have been cliques. A clique consists of people who all interact with each other but have no common links to anyone else. Cliques may form on the basis of shared demographic characteristics that are relatively rare in a particular organizational setting (Mehra et al., 1998). The effects of cliques on individuals in the clique (in terms of individual-level issues such as motivation and work performance) and on organizational functioning (in terms of organizational-level issues such as knowledge gathering and dissemination) are still relatively little studied, however.

Business Unit Level of Observation

As an organization expands into a heterogeneous environment (such as a different country), it is likely to establish a business unit focused on the complexities of that environment. Such business units, despite remaining part of the overall multidivisional enterprise, may achieve semi-autonomous status. Formal mechanisms exist to coordinate the activities of such business units (see Thompson, 1967), but social networks are just as likely to play a role here as they are at the interpersonal level. The study of the social networks that spring up between business units can inform us concerning how important resources are hoarded or shared, and why some units are likely to succeed whereas others may fail. The networks of interest include, but are not limited to, inter-unit work flow, personnel exchange, resource exchange and knowledge-sharing.

Complex organizations comprising different units operating in different environments can therefore be conceptualized as differentiated networks. These networks of business units succeed or fail depending on how well the network shares expertise, learning and resources among the interacting units (Ghoshal and Bartlett, 1990). The challenge for the individual business unit is to compete both within the internal economy of the firm for resources, and to differentiate itself in the external environment where it may face a range of specialized competitors. Thus the patterns of internal links (Nohria and Ghoshal, 1997) within the organization and external links (Tsai, 2001) to resource providers in the larger environment may be crucial to survival and profitability.

The examination of internal and external ties of business units has barely begun. We do have some information about tie formation between business units, and the effects of such ties on business unit performance. Within the multi-unit firm, business units that are more central in the resource exchange network are quicker than other units to establish inter-unit resource exchanges with newly-formed units (Tsai, 2000). Business units that exchange resources with many other units tend to produce a higher number of product innovations (Tsai and Ghoshal, 1998). Social ties between units facilitate knowledge sharing for units that compete in the same market segments (Tsai, 2002). Strong ties between business units facilitate the transfer of complex knowledge (whereas weak ties are sufficient for less complex knowledge) (Hansen, 1999). Business unit performance can be positively affected by the business unit leader's network of ties with the dominant coalition of people who run the overall firm (Mehra et al., 2002).

Issues of power and dependence have tended to be neglected in network treatments of firms. The multi-unit firm can be considered a political economy in which some units are more dominant than others (see Benson, 1975). The distribution of scarce resources in such an economy can be controlled by a dominant block of units associated with a ruling family or ethnic group, raising the question of how a business unit can garner scarce resources in such an environment (see Tsai and Kilduff, 2002). Given the existence of allied groups or blocks of business units within the multi-unit firm, research is needed concerning how individual units compete for resources such as knowledge and personnel. Should individual units focus on establishing and maintaining resource exchange ties with other units within their own block, or should units cross block boundaries to forge ties with units in other blocks? These questions remain to be answered.

Organizational Level of Observation

We have known for a long time that organizations form ties with one another in competitive marketplaces. Adam Smith famously decried the tendency of 'people of the same trade' to engage in 'a conspiracy against the public, or in some contrivance to raise prices' (Smith, 1979: 232–33). Although legal constraints prohibit large competitors from monopolizing markets through collusion, ties between organizations include strategic alliances (e.g., Gulati, 1995), buyer–supplier relationships (e.g., Dyer and Singh, 1998), and joint ventures (e.g., Hamel et al., 1989). To some extent, the contemporary landscape of small firm cooperation resembles that of the pre-industrial revolution. The economist's classical market of well-bounded autonomous firms engaged in utility maximization has been overlaid with networks of trust-based exchange – networks that characterized trade and enterprise throughout most of human history up to the seventeenth century (Tilly, 2001). Firms in knowledge-based industries that fail to establish requisite connections with other industry firms may suffer from the 'liability of unconnectedness' – a reduced capacity to participate in the ongoing processes of learning and innovation that lead to firm growth (Powell et al., 1996).

The interesting interorganizational network questions concern the consequences of different patterns of social ties among firms (e.g., Davis, 1991). We need to know more about how embeddedness within networks of ties can constrain and enable firm behaviour: What mix of arms' length and strong ties can benefit firms (see Baker, 1990; Uzzi, 1996)? Under what circumstances do competitors cooperate? What are some of the perils for firms of allowing current interorganizational links to largely determine future links (see Gulati and Gargiulo, 1999)? These questions direct attention to the mix of cooperation and competition that has come to characterize firm behaviour in the twenty-first century.

Other Levels of Observation

We envisage and encourage organizational social network research involving relationships among different tasks, routines, grammars and processes. Already researchers have explored novel units of analysis within social network frameworks. For example, an analysis of the patent citation network in the worldwide semiconductor industry investigated the competitive crowding and status of semiconductor firms (Podolny et al., 1996). Cross-level analyses are also beginning to appear, and can help inform us concerning how actors integrate and replicate higher-level structures. For example, an individual who appears to be isolated at one level of analysis, such as the team, may emerge as a key link between teams when another level of analysis, such as the whole organization, is studied (e.g., Weimann, 1982). We focus in this book not on levels of analysis but on substantive topics of research that have implications across levels. One of the beauties of network approaches to organizational studies is the extent to which the same network topics and methods apply at different levels.

MAPPING THE CHAPTERS IN THE BOOK

As enthusiasm for social network methods and approaches has grown in the field of organizational research, major debates concerning the scope, distinctiveness, and theoretical importance of social network thinking have tended to be neglected. Sometimes it appears that the network paradigm is in danger of becoming a victim of its own success – invoked by practically every organizational researcher, included in almost every analysis, and yet strangely absent as a distinctive set of ideas. Some organizational scholars have criticized social network research as mainly descriptive, method-driven, atheoretical and static. We seek to capture the distinctiveness of social network methods and ideas, and to address major debates concerning network theory, the treatment of the individual, dynamic analysis and cross-disciplinary trends. We view social network research in organizations as a changing set of approaches that can and should be guided by theory, operate across levels, investigate processes over time, and engage itself at the cutting edge of contemporary thinking.

This book is written for those interested in organizational social network research – understanding it, engaging in it, critiquing it and enjoying it. No previous familiarity with network concepts is assumed. We introduce and explain network thinking and provide a glossary of technical terms. The book is written so that even abstruse methods and complex ideas are accessible to all. We have incorporated examples throughout the book and provided a set of exercises in the appendix to illustrate and explore social network concepts and analysis. The six chapters that follow this chapter introduce concepts and methods, evaluate the claims of network theory, tackle the vexed question of network treatments of individuals, propose a process approach to network dynamics, outline how network research can move beyond the constraints of the current structuralist paradigm, and conclude with a summary of what we have learned.

More specifically, in Chapter 2 we provide an overview of social network research, highlighting (for organizational research) distinctive aspects of social network approaches and outlining the major orienting concepts. The distinctiveness of network approaches derives from their focus on relations between actors, their ability to address multi-level issues, and their integration of quantitative, qualitative and graphical data. Orienting concepts include the embeddedness of work-related and economic transactions in patterns of social relations, social capital as a set of resources inherent in an actor's set of network ties, and structural holes as gaps between actors or groups of actors that share no direct ties. At the level of the whole network, important concepts include the density of ties, the centralization of the network, the reachability of actors in the network, and the extent to which network relations are balanced. At the level of the individual tie, important concepts include strength, reciprocity and multiplexity of ties. In this and subsequent chapters we are careful to place contemporary work in a historical context, showcasing such classics of organizational network research as Bruce Kapferer's analyses of interaction, change and conflict in an African factory.

In Chapter 3, we ask whether the network approach can claim to be something more than a collection of methods. What are the major claimants to the title of social network theory applicable to organizations? We look at network approaches that have been borrowed, invented and exported. Specifically, we investigate borrowings from mathematics (graph theory) and social psychology (e.g., balance theory); home-grown network theory (e.g., weak tie and structural hole approaches); and exports of network ideas into other organization theories (e.g., hybrid resource dependence and network theory). Our purpose in Chapter 3 is to review and integrate diverse strands of thinking as a foundation for more theory-driven research in the area of organizational social networks.

In Chapter 4, we move to deeper theoretical issues regarding how individual attributes should be studied in conjunction with the more structural emphasis characteristic of network analysis. Some network researchers have not just ignored individual actors, they have disparaged any attempt to understand how individuals help shape the networks within which they are embedded. Indeed, there seems to be a structural hole between those who focus on social networks and those who focus on the attributes of individuals. In bridging across this structural hole, we address issues of individual difference from a network perspective, and outline two emerging theoretical approaches: cognitive network theory, and an emergent theory of personality and social structure. Cognitive network theory builds from the classic work of Lewin and Heider and includes consideration of cognitive balance, cognitive accuracy and cognitive maps. From this distinctive perspective, the organization can be understood as a network of cognitions. The emergent personality approach to social structure investigates whether individuals' personality orientations (such as self-monitoring) affect the structuring of social ties in organizations.

In Chapter 5 we tackle the difficult issue of network change over time, introducing the twin processes of serendipity and goal-directedness to understand how different organizational trajectories unfold. Whereas one process (goal-directedness) is teleological, subordinating actors' interests and interactions to explicit goals, the other process (serendipity) involves no pre-existing goals, featuring growth through dyadic matching, with more decentralized structures and more diverse actors. We illustrate these processes with analyses of two networks.

In Chapter 6 we ask whether social network research should go boldly where it has never gone before: taking ideas and directions from the raft of poststructuralist approaches that have coursed through other areas of social science and the humanities. We examine the implications for social network research of the poststructuralist critique of network assumptions, and investigate possible elaborations of network research in such directions as pluralism, fluidity, subjectivity and society as text.

Finally, in Chapter 7 we summarize what we have learned and what still needs to be done.

SUMMARY

This book reflects our own view of what is important in social network research. Instead of providing just a review of existing research, we have opened up dialogue on a range of new approaches. We think that debate and controversy are good for social science in that they encourage a more rapid development of theory and research. Social network research has the potential to contribute far beyond the range of issues that currently preoccupies the field. Our book aims to capture the allure of network thinking and marry it to the promise of new theoretical ideas to provide a platform from which innovative research can proceed.

RECOMMENDED FURTHER READING

Baker, W.E. 2000. *Achieving success through social capital.* San Francisco: Jossey-Bass.
This practitioner-oriented guide to the acquisition and use of social capital draws extensively from research and theory concerning interpersonal social networks.

Baker, W.E. and Faulkner, R.R. 2002. Interorganizational networks. In J.A.C. Baum (ed.), *The Blackwell companion to organizations*, pp. 520–40. Oxford: Blackwell.
Surveys research and new directions on networks involving organizations at several levels of analysis: dyad, triad, organization set, and organization field.

Brass, D.J. 1995. A social network perspective on human resources management. In Gerald R. Ferris (ed.), *Research in personnel and human resources management*, 13: 39–79. Greenwich, CT: JAI Press.
Lucid guide to social network concepts and their potential application to research on a range of human resource topics such as recruitment, training, and performance appraisal.

Krackhardt, D. and Brass, D.J. 1994. Intraorganizational networks: The micro side. In S. Wasserman and J. Galaskiewicz (eds), *Advances in social network analysis*, pp. 207–29. Thousand Oaks, CA: Sage.

Survey of how network research can be used to bring new insights to such traditional micro-OB topics as motivation, leadership, job design, turnover/absenteeism, and work attitudes.

Powell, W.W. and Smith-Doerr, L. 1994. Networks and economic life. In N.J. Smelser and R. Swedberg (eds), *The handbook of economic sociology*, **pp. 368–402. Princeton, NJ: Princeton University Press.**

Broad-ranging survey of research on topics that include power and influence (e.g., resource dependence, social class), the firm as a network of treaties (e.g., communication networks within organizations, transfer of tacit knowledge), and networks of production (e.g., regional networks, business groups).

The network concept is one of the defining paradigms of the modern era. In fields as different as physics, biology, linguistics, anthropology, sociology and psychotherapy, network ideas have been repeatedly invoked over the last hundred years. The network approach allows researchers to capture the interactions of any individual unit within the larger field of activity to which the unit belongs.

The multiple origins of network approaches for the social sciences contribute to the eclecticism that characterizes current work. Briefly stated, network ideas flowed into the social sciences from three main sources. First, German researchers (such as Kurt Lewin, Fritz Heider and Jacob Moreno), influenced by developments in field theory in physics, transferred the network idea to the examination of social interaction. These scientists brought their distinctive new approach to the USA during the 1920s and 1930s. Network research on cognition and interpersonal influence originates with the influential traditions of Lewin and Heider.

Secondly, the influence of a mathematical approach to social interaction, evident in Kurt Lewin's work, was taken up in the USA first by researchers working with graph theory (e.g., Cartwright and Harary, 1956), and later by a Harvard group working with Harrison White. This emphasis on mathematics helped transform the study of social networks from description to analysis. With the advent of powerful computers, the promise of the network approach began to be realized: individual units within social fields could be simultaneously analysed to discover new insights concerning social structure and interaction.

The third main source of network ideas in the social sciences derived not from mathematically-inclined sociologists but from anthropologically-inclined organizational fieldworkers. In the USA, a group based in the Harvard Business School began in the 1920s a ten-year series of anthropological investigations of factory life in the Hawthorne works of the Western Electric Company of Chicago. The famous Hawthorne Studies were the first to use sociograms to diagram the structure of freely-chosen social interactions. Thus, from the very beginning, social network analysis had its roots in organizational settings.

The Hawthorne researchers were not the only anthropologically-inclined researchers who contributed to the developing science of social networks in organizational settings. A British tradition, centred around the Department of Social Anthropology at Manchester University, inspired innovative examinations of organizational conflict from a social network perspective. In particular, Bruce Kapferer's analyses of social interaction, change, and conflict in African work-places such as a garment factory (1972) advanced the practice and the science of social network research. Kapferer, following the innovative social community research of his mentors, such as Barnes, Mitchell and Bott, collected data on the interactions of every employee of an Indian-owned clothing factory in the Zambian town of Kabwe. He tested a series of hypotheses derived from exchange theory (Blau, 1964) rather than resting content with a purely descriptive account of factory life. He examined how the social networks of interaction changed over time in relation to significant events occurring in the factory. Thus, Kapferer was able to examine a complete network of interaction over time and relate it to sub-stantively interesting organizational issues. It's worth spending a little time on Kapferer's exemplary research because it illustrates both the history of the net-work approach and also the contemporary possibilities for analysis. To assist readers in following the technical terms used in this discussion and in the rest of the book, we provide a glossary of terms at the end of the book.

Kapferer emphasized that the social composition of the factory was an emer-gent property of choices and decisions made by interacting individuals. He charted the changes in social networks by collecting network data at three points in time. From these data he computed network measures of the extent to which employees achieved organizational power and influence through being able to access and mobilize people in the factory, anticipating current theoretical work on how individuals' networks can span across social divides (e.g., Burt, 1992).

The most dramatic innovation in Kapferer's work was his use of social network data to predict strike activity by the workers. Figures 2.1 and 2.2 depict the instrumental network in the factory at two points in time. The instrumen-tal network was defined as including such transactional activities as 'lending or giving money, assistance at times of personal crisis and help at work' (Kapferer, 1972: 164). He excluded activities that were mandated by the production process itself. At the end of time 1 some senior workers organized walkouts to try to secure wage and work improvements, but their efforts failed to gain the support of many of the skilled and unskilled workers, and thus ultimately were

FIGURE 2.1

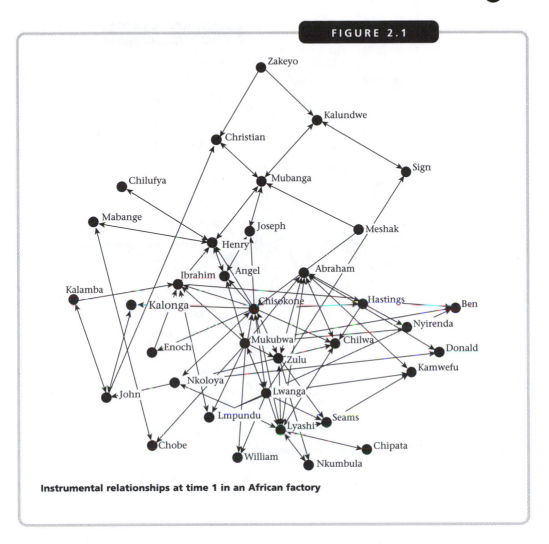

Instrumental relationships at time 1 in an African factory

deemed a failure. Note the relatively dispersed leadership structure evident in Figure 2.1: the graph has a relatively low degree centralization index of .28, indicating the absence of informal leaders around whom the other employees are organized (Scott, 2000: 89). Degree centralization is a measure that varies between 0 and 1 with higher values indicating a greater degree of centralization around a central point or points. Figure 2.2 shows that degree centralization increased to .45 at the time of the second data collection, seven months later, indicating a much greater influence of leaders on followers.

Simply put, between time 1 and time 2, Kapferer's data show that the factory workers were 'more linked into a common set of interactional relationships' (1972: 180). Relative to time 1, ties at time 2 tended to cross-cut the

FIGURE 2.2

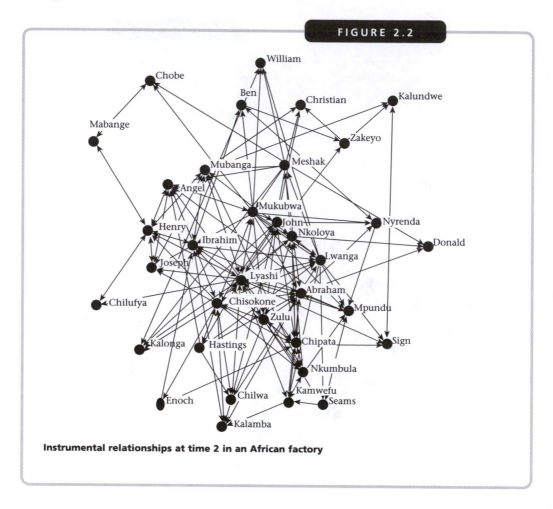

Instrumental relationships at time 2 in an African factory

different clusters in the factory, tended to be multiplex, and tended to show the senior workers in the factory exerting a greater degree of power and influence. This greater solidarity among the different factions allowed the factory workers to take the decisive action to go on strike in February 1965 in support of a claim for a £1 increase in wages.

Kapferer's work is exemplary in its combination of network data and ethnographic detail. In particular, Kapferer places the interactions within the factory in a richly-observed context of recreational activities, kinship, marriage and local politics. He interprets the meaning of his quantitative data matrices through his detailed knowledge of each specific person in the matrix, and their activities. For example, one central person in Kapferer's analysis is Lyashi, a tailor, who attempted to achieve a position of power and influence in the informal network of relationships. Figures 2.1 and 2.2 show that Lyashi succeeded over the seven-month period in moving from a relatively peripheral position in the instrumental network to the most central position. The book presents many details concerning Lyashi and his daily life, including such relevant extra-curricular information as this: 'Although the Lumpa Church [of which he was once a Deacon] is banned, ... he maintains a vast network of ties with other "erstwhile" members of the movement' (Kapferer, 1972: 214).

Around the time Kapferer's book was published, articles were beginning to appear in organizational journals containing analyses of communication flows. One of the first of these was a description of communication in a research and development laboratory showing diagrams of social contacts and some simple statistics (Allen and Cohen, 1969). The focus in this article and similar articles by others (e.g., Pettigrew, 1972) was on the role of sociometric stars and gate-keepers in brokering information, a focus that has been rediscovered by the recent literature on structural holes (e.g., Burt, 1992).

Surprisingly, these interesting and innovative analyses by Kapferer and others made no use of the technical developments in graph theory applied to organizational settings decades earlier. George Homans (1950) had illustrated the usefulness of rearranging the rows and columns of data matrices to reveal underlying structure. Systematic applications of matrix algebra to sociometric data had been described in the social science literature (e.g., Festinger, 1949; Forsyth and Katz, 1946). One of the earliest applications of these new matrix techniques to an organizational data set was published in the *American Sociological Review* (Weiss and Jacobson, 1955). The authors collected data from 196 members of a government agency in interviews lasting from one to three hours. The sociometric questions related to the workflow network – that is, the people each individual had worked with over the past few months. As part of the structural analysis, the authors reordered rows and columns to produce separate blocks of highly-connected workers. The final analysis allowed the identification of work groups, liaison persons between groups, and people with no work contacts – the isolates. The authors mention the possibility of relating structural indicators such as individual centrality in the network to outcome variables such as organizational identification, but no data are reported. The wholesale application of the new social network methods to organizational data had to await the availability of relatively cheap computing power.

DISTINCTIVE FEATURES OF THE SOCIAL NETWORK APPROACH

One of the attractive features of the social network approach to organizations is the potential to analyse network relations with an ever-expanding range of algorithms, programs, and procedures that map closely on to important orienting concepts and characteristics of networks. Comprehensive reviews of network methods are available (e.g., Wasserman and Faust, 1994), as are introductory handbooks (e.g., Degenne and Forse, 1999; Schensul et al., 1999; Scott, 2000). In this section, we offer examples to illustrate commonly used network methods and we discuss distinctive features of the social network approach.

For the sake of simplicity we will assume that we want to gather information on friendship ties between individuals in a small organization of 33 people. How do we do this? There are at least three ways of proceeding. First, we could collect *whole network* data using a roster of the names of all 33 people in the organization. We could list the names on a sheet of paper with instructions to the respondent to tick the names of those individuals whom the respondent considers to be his or her personal friends. From these data we could then prepare a 'whole' network of relations that indicated for each pair of individuals whether one or both of the individuals considered the other to be a friend. The data could be arranged in a 33 by 33 asymmetric matrix.

But what if we were unable to gain access to all 33 people? An alternative would be to collect egocentric data from each person available to us. This would entail a significant sacrifice in data quality. Each individual that agreed to participate could be prompted to give us the names of his or her friends in the organization. This prompting could take the form of a complete roster of 33 names. Or we could prompt the individual to remember by providing cues such as different roles ('Do you have any friends who are managers?'). Once the respondent provided a list of names, the respondent could then be asked to indicate the relations between the friends: Which of the respondent's friends were friends of each other? From these data, each respondent's position in the egocentric network could be estimated. This approach seems particularly suitable for very large organizations where it is impossible to gain data from all organizational members.

A third approach bypasses the individual members of the organization completely and relies on archival records. Personnel records, for example, often contain a wealth of information concerning whom job applicants know in the organization, who is kin with whom, who recommended who for employment, and so on (see Burt and Ronchi, 1990, for a brilliant example of this strategy). Records of relationships such as friendship and kinship are collected for a range of different purposes and often form the basis of pioneering work on social networks. See, for example, Uzzi's (1996) work on the garment manufacturing industry, utilizing records collected by the Ladies Garment Workers' Union, and Padgett and Ansell's (1993) work on the Medici family, utilizing records maintained for hundreds of years. Archival records are particularly useful in cases where it may be dangerous to approach respondents, or where respondents are unlikely to respond to questionnaires.

Each approach, therefore, has its uses. What can be done with these data once they are arranged in matrices? In the case of whole network data, collected by the use of roster-type questionnaires or through archival records, an almost unlimited range of analytical techniques can be employed. The centrality of each actor in the network can be analysed on several indices (e.g., Brass, 1984) including indegree (i.e., how popular the actor is), betweenness (i.e., the extent to which the actor functions as a go-between for others not directly connected), and eigenvector (i.e., the extent which the actor is connected to others who are highly central). The network can be analysed to see how many and what kinds of clique exist, whether these cliques overlap, and the extent to which each dyadic pair in the network belongs to the same cliques (e.g., Krackhardt, 1999). The network can be analysed into blocks of actors similar on the basis of their ties to other actors. And of course, the whole network itself can be correlated with another matrix of information about these actors such as a matrix of correlations showing how similar each pair of actors is with respect to attitudes or behaviours (e.g., Kilduff, 1992).

At its best, network research has several distinctive features that differentiate it from traditional approaches in the social sciences: (1) Network research focuses on relations and the patterns of relations rather than on attributes of actors; (2) Network research is amenable to multiple levels of analysis, and can thus provide micro–macro linkages; (3) Network research can integrate quantitative, qualitative and graphical data, allowing more thorough and in-depth analysis. None of these features is well established in traditional approaches in the social sciences.

Relations and Patterns of Relations

The network approach can test whether the pattern of network ties in a particular social world is related to other important patterns such as the pattern of decision-making. Let's look at one simplified example from the research literature. The research question was whether individuals, in making important decisions, tended to be influenced by their friends. The author collected data from 170 MBA students at Cornell University by asking them to look carefully down a list of their classmates and check off the names of those they considered to be personal friends. From these data a square matrix (known as an adjacency matrix) was constructed showing for each pair of people in the sample whether one considered the other to be a friend. One row in the matrix showed for an individual all of those he or she had chosen as friends. A section of such a matrix is illustrated in Figure 2.3. In the first row we can see that Dana has reported that she is friends with Bill and Cy. If we look at the rows for these two, we see that Bill fails to reciprocate Dana's friendship nomination, but that Cy does reciprocate. Thus, the matrix contains *asymmetric* data.

Each individual in the sample signed up for one or more interviews with the 120 companies recruiting at the school. The number of interviews each person could sign up for was restricted by a points system. All of the sign-up information was available for public inspection on bulletin boards, and was

FIGURE 2.3

	Dana	Bill	Ed	June	Cy	Red	Sue	Joe	.....
Dana		1			1				
Bill								1	
Ed	1			1		1	1		
June			1		1				
Cy	1			1					
Red			1					1	
Sue			1					1	

Adjacency matrix showing who is friends with whom

also archived on the computer. Thus it was possible to create another matrix (known as an incidence matrix) showing for all 120 companies which ones each individual had signed up with. The matrix had 170 rows (one for each person) and 120 columns (one for each company). The methodological question was: How could we compare each person with every other person in terms of how similar their decision-making was? The answer was to correlate each row with every other row so that for any two people in the sample we knew precisely how similar their decision-making was in this one important arena of organizational choice.

Figure 2.4 illustrates the similarity matrix that resulted from this procedure. For each pair of people in the sample there is a correlation expressing how similar their choices were across the 120 recruiting companies. Note that this matrix is necessarily *symmetric*. Once this matrix was created it was possible to ask whether individuals' patterns of behaviours were similar to those of their friends. In the research article this question was answered in the affirmative through the use of a non-parametric regression analysis that controlled for alternative explanations, and took into account the non-independence of the data (Kilduff, 1990). The basis of this analysis, however, derives from whether the '1s' in Figure 2.3 are in the same cells as the high correlations in Figure 2.4.

FIGURE 2.4

	Dana	Bill	Ed	June	Cy	Red	Sue	Joe	.....
Dana		.49	.13	.01	.22	−.04	−.06	.09	
Bill	.49		.10	−.05	.03	.07	.09	.37	
Ed	.13	.10		.56	−.07	.33	.25	.06	
June	.01	−.05	.56		.22	.10	−.08	.15	
Cy	.22	.03	−.07	.22		.09	.04	.12	
Red	−.04	.07	.33	.10	.09		−.09	.19	
Sue	−.06	.09	.25	−.08	.04	−.09		.44	

Similarity matrix showing the correlation of each pair's interview selections

Much network research explores *social structures*, defined as 'patterns of connectivity and cleavage within social systems' (Wellman, 1988b: 26). Social structures are abstract representations of patterns of relationships between actors (Nadel, 1957: 12). Studying social structures helps us to understand the ways in which groups of actors cluster together in social space (e.g., Burt, 1978). Emergent structures can be compared with other structural depictions of the same actors to determine, for example, the degree of overlap between observed structure and a structure derived from theory (e.g., Barley, 1990). Network research can analyse both the whole system of relations and parts of the system simultaneously: 'Analysts are therefore able to trace lateral and vertical flows of information, identify sources and targets and detect structural constraints operating on flows of resources' (Wellman, 1988b: 26). This ability to capture the structure of the whole interacting system and its constituent parts in one analysis makes the social network approach particularly attractive to students of organizations.

Let's look at a specific example of how the network approach reveals social structure. As the examples in Figures 2.3 and 2.4 illustrate, individuals connected to the same organizations are, in a sense, connected to each other through those organizations. In the same way, organizations are connected to each other through the people they attract as members. Thus, social structure

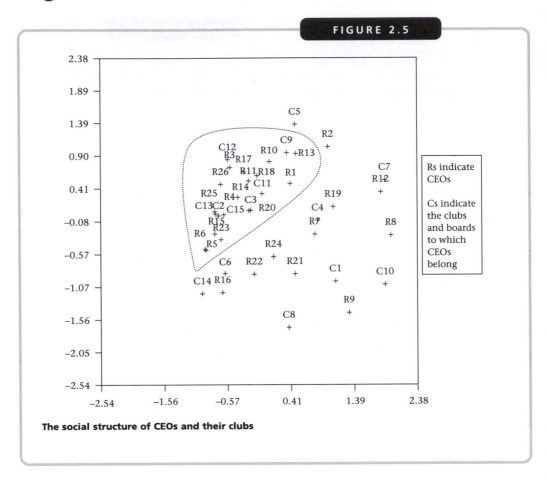

FIGURE 2.5

The social structure of CEOs and their clubs

involving people and organizations has a dual quality: people are connected to each other through organizations and organizations are connected to each other through people (Breiger, 1974). To illustrate this point we turn to a celebrated data set collected by Galaskiewicz (1985) showing the affiliations of 26 Minneapolis area CEOs to 15 clubs and corporate boards.

Figure 2.5 models both the CEOs' and their organizational affiliations in the same analytical space using a technique called correspondence analysis that uses an objective criterion to display optimally the correlations among two sets of entities. (For more information on this type of analysis and its application to these particular data, see Wasserman and Faust, 1994: 334–42.) The display in Figure 2.5 shows what appears to be a core set of CEOs who meet each other at a core set of clubs and boards, forming an elite structure, with other CEOs dispersed around the periphery. The core people and clubs (contained within the heart-shaped dotted line) are clustered around members such as R4 and R14 and they attend clubs such as C3 and C15. We could perform many other structural analyses on these data to check how the CEOs cluster together, and whether the dominance structure suggested by Figure 2.5 was supported.

Micro–Macro Linkages

This example of social structural analysis illustrates how the social network approach helps us understand micro–macro linkages in organizations. A hypothetical example of such linkages is illustrated in Figure 2.6 that borrows from the so-called bathtub model developed by James Coleman (1990: 8). In the figure, the overall social network of relationships involving CEOs and their clubs is hypothesized to influence the individual connections that CEOs make (link 1), and these individual connections are predicted to affect the actions that individual CEOs take (link 2). These actions, in turn, may contribute to the dominance by an elite group of CEOs over the distribution of resources within the community (link 3). Also shown is the direct link between the whole network of CEOs and elite dominance across the top of the figure. Thus, the network approach can help us understand the ways in which individuals affect institutional outcomes and how larger social structures affect individuals. (See Huber, 1991, for a general treatment of this issue.) Note also that network analysis helps delineate such structural features of organizational contexts as the density of social ties (Alba, 1982: 40). Structural features such as density derive from interactions among individuals, and these emergent structures can be used to interpret individual behaviours.

The social structures that emerge from network analyses constitute social realities of which the social actors themselves may not be aware (Galaskiewicz, 1996: 21). Social structure is often not obvious because it involves a complex meshing of different types of network ties that may span across different levels of analysis and may have accumulated over many years. For example, a network analysis of the social relationships in one conflict-ridden factory revealed patterns of kinship and dependence formed over the 30-year life of the factory that were unknown to many of the key actors involved (Burt and Ronchi, 1990). Social network research has an *emancipatory potential* in that it can inform actors of non-obvious constraints and opportunities inherent in patterns of social connections. Part of the increasing popular interest in the results of social network research derives from this potential.

An Integration of Quantitative, Qualitative and Graphical Data

Another distinctive aspect of the social network approach that we have exploited in this chapter is its ability to supplement quantitative analysis with qualitative and graphical data. Traditional social science research tends to focus

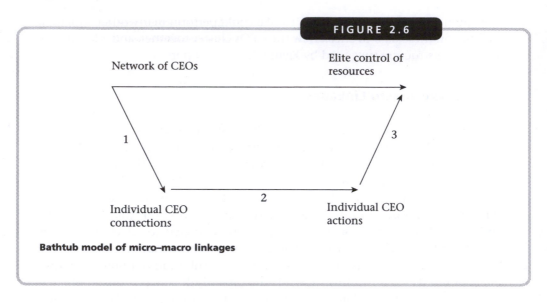

FIGURE 2.6

Bathtub model of micro–macro linkages

on mean differences between groups. Thus, data analysis proceeds at a high level of abstraction. But social network research enables the researcher to stay close to the data. For example, an ethnographic study of the conversations between radiologists and technologists in two hospitals was supplemented with extensive analyses and representations of the social ties between occupants of different roles (Barley, 1990). Similarly, a quantitative analysis of the marginality of underrepresented groups was visually reinforced by a network depiction of friendship ties between individuals (Mehra et al., 1998). In both these examples, the network pictures added a degree of realism largely lacking in the regression tables of the typical journal article.

An excellent example of the power of a network sociogram to supplement quantitative analysis is provided in Figure 2.7 that shows interactions among 14 participants and four instructors at a National Science Foundation summer camp in 1992 (see Borgatti et al., 1999, for more details). The research question is: To what extent do people's interactions exhibit *homophily*, specifically a tendency to interact with similar others such as members of their own sex (see McPherson et al., 2001, for a review)? This question can be addressed quantitatively, but the diagram also provides clear evidence. The sexes tend to clump together in recognizable groups, with the only exception being the female Brazey who has attached herself to the group that includes the four instructors (Steve, Bert, Russ and Gery). Note also how the diagram clearly illustrates the strategic importance of *cutpoints*: actors (like John and Holly) who constitute the only links between different groups. (See Brass, 1985, for a similar example of gender homophily.)

In yet another example of how network diagrams serve analytical purposes, the main burden of proof in one research article was carried by a series of depictions

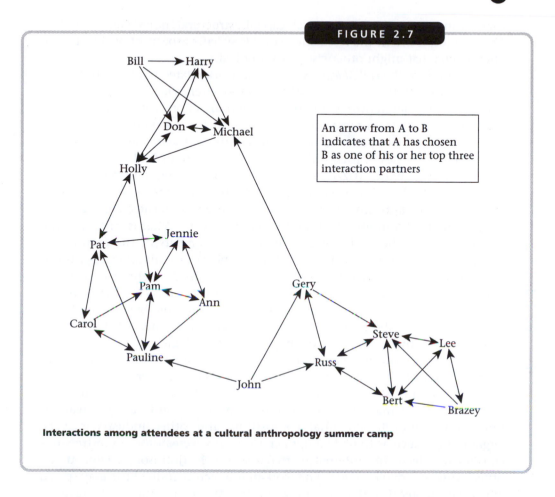

FIGURE 2.7

An arrow from A to B indicates that A has chosen B as one of his or her top three interaction partners

Interactions among attendees at a cultural anthropology summer camp

of the various ways in which individuals misperceived their own friendship networks in organizations (Kumbasar et al., 1994). The network approach enables the analyst to retain the richness of the data rather than having to sacrifice richness for statistical power.

MAJOR CONCEPTS IN SOCIAL NETWORK RESEARCH

Orienting Concepts

As we have alluded to in the discussion up to this point, the social network approach to organizations is premised on the importance of several concepts that include embeddedness, social capital, structural holes and centrality. These concepts orient the researcher towards specific aspects of organizational phenomena that might otherwise be overlooked.

According to the *embeddedness* argument, work-related transactions tend to overlap with patterns of social relations (Granovetter, 1985). Thus, business is embedded in social networks, and patterns of transactions within and between firms may depart from what might be expected from a pure economic perspective. People may prefer to do business with contractors and others with whom they have ties of friendship or kinship rather than find exchange partners in the open market (Uzzi, 1996). One example from our own research (Tsai and Kilduff, 2002) is displayed in Figure 2.8. The figure shows how important knowledge, such as technological advances, were communicated among the 36 business units in a multi-billion dollar food company. What is striking is the extent to which the 14 business units run by members of the family that founded the company tended to be the central players in this knowledge transfer network. The family-run units tend to cluster in the central area of the knowledge transfer network. These units tended to favour each other with new knowledge, and also tended to receive new knowledge from business units run by non-family members. Knowledge transfer was, in fact, embedded in kinship relationships rather than following purely economic logic.

Some organizations may suffer from a 'liability of unconnectedness' (Powell et al., 1996) in the sense that organizational members fail to develop strong bonds of trust to important actors inside and outside the organization. Top management may even punish those who create links across organizational boundaries to potential competitors and other industry players. Organizations such as Digital Equipment Company were notorious fortress-like cultures in which 'the internal mattered so much' (Johnson, 1996). At the other extreme, a dynamic social network of interacting individuals may span a whole geographical area threatening the traditional hegemony of organizational boundaries. As one executive of a Silicon Valley company commented: 'There's far greater loyalty to one's craft than to one's company. ... A company is just a vehicle which allows you to work' (Saxenian, 1990: 97). Resource flows within organizations are likely to depart from what a purely economic model would predict, according to the embeddedness argument. People are likely to favour their family and friends with timely information, recommendations, interesting projects and other career-building opportunities. The path to advancement may be embedded in social relationships. Just having a contact in an organization can enhance the chances of being offered a job (Fernandez and Weinberg, 1997) and can significantly increase salary negotiation outcomes (Seidel et al., 2000).

This emphasis on the importance of social relationships is summarized in the concept of *social capital*. This concept can be defined, at the individual actor level, as the potential resources inherent in an actor's set of social ties. In one of the first uses of the term in the network literature, social capital was

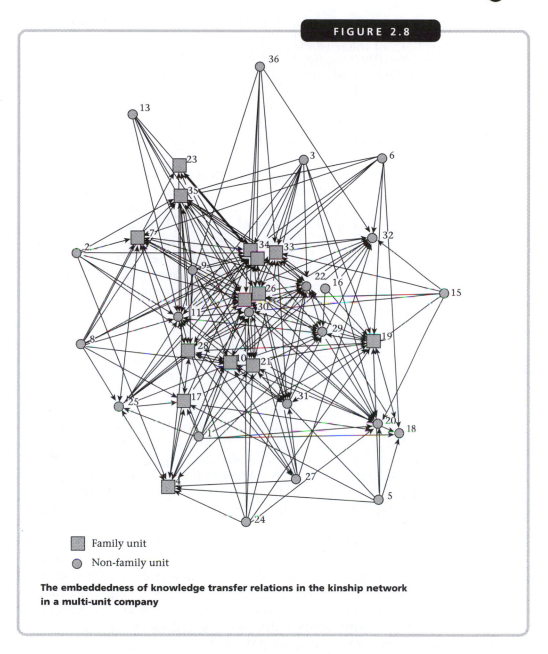

FIGURE 2.8

■ Family unit

● Non-family unit

The embeddedness of knowledge transfer relations in the kinship network in a multi-unit company

described as 'personal investments' that could be used for economic advantage by the activation of 'particular links in a social network' (Mitchell, 1974: 286). Used in this sense of a personal investment, social capital can be traded for other types of capital such as money or cultural capital (Bourdieu, 1980).

Personal connections can be useful in facilitating access to jobs (Granovetter, 1974) and promotions (Brass, 1984; Burt, 1992). The social network approach assumes that different configurations of social ties produce different benefits for actors (Burt, 2000). Social capital is often described as different from money and other types of capital in that it inheres in the relationships between people. Actors do not control their social capital in the same way they control their money or their human capital. To use social capital, it is necessary to draw upon the cooperation of another actor by, for example, asking for advice or help at work.

Social capital can also be defined as the benefits that accrue to the collectivity as a result of the maintenance of positive relations between different groups, organizational units or hierarchical levels (e.g., Burt and Ronchi, 1990; Tsai 2000; Tsai and Ghoshal, 1998). One of the unexplored aspects of social capital concerns how the individual use of personal connections to further egoistic ends can undermine collective social capital (Portes, 2000: 4).

From the beginnings of social network research, there has been a fascination with ways in which the absence of ties between individuals defines both the structure of networks and the opportunities to build social capital. The large literature on balance theory, for example, investigates the puzzling absence of ties between people who have friends in common (e.g., Holland and Leinhardt, 1977). The pioneering work on blockmodelling aimed to discover, in any social network, the zero-blocks, that is, the groups between which there are few or no connections (Lorrain and White, 1971). This latter work has led directly to the current interest in *structural holes*, which are gaps in the social world across which there are no current connections, but that can be connected by savvy entrepreneurs who thereby gain control over the flow of information across the gaps (Burt, 1992). Individual actors (people, sub-units, organizations) have been portrayed as seeking to increase their social capital by performing the *liaison* role of connecting two otherwise disconnected cliques, or by *bridging* from one group to which they belong to another group that they join.

Structural-hole research focuses attention on the importance of these liaison and bridging ties. According to this perspective, actors can leverage their investments in social relations by establishing relations with a diverse set of groups (preferably groups that are not connected to each other) rather than establishing all of their relationships with members of one group. For example, in Figure 2.7, Holly spans across a structural hole in establishing the only connections between two different sub-groups.

A recent influential study of the effects of structural-hole spanning on outcomes included an analysis of the self-reported networks of managers of a large high-technology firm. The managers' networks were divided into different types of structure (entrepreneurial, clique and hierarchical) depending on the kinds of ties that the managers described as existing between the people they were connected to in the organization (see also Tichy, 1973, for a useful typology of cliques). Entrepreneurial networks tended to be rich in structural holes: there were about 13 reported contacts with a low density of connection among the contacts. Clique networks tended to be constrained in the sense that the individuals' contacts were themselves connected to each other. The clique networks were smaller than the entrepreneurial networks (about nine contacts) and everyone in the network was reported by the respondent to be close or especially close to everyone else. Thus, these were cliques in the strict sense of the term. Hierarchical networks tended to be the same size as clique networks, but had a low reported density, with many of the reported ties branching out from one or a few people. The research found that high-ranking males who were promoted early tended to describe networks that were entre- preneurial, whereas women and lower-ranking men who were promoted early described networks that were hierarchical (Burt, 1992).

In general, therefore, early promotion was associated with a low density of contacts among the people in the manager's self-reported circle. The research was unable, however, to determine whether low density caused early promo- tions, or whether those people promoted early developed less dense relation- ships as a consequence of the promotion from one level to another (see discussion in Burt, 1992: 173–80). Previous research in a publishing company showed that promotions of non-supervisors to supervisory positions were significantly influenced by the extent to which individuals spanned across structural holes in the departmental communication networks (Brass, 1984). This study was longitudinal, over a three-year period, and therefore avoided the cross-sectional problems associated with Burt (1992). A follow-up study to Burt's, using similar methodology, attempted to correct for the possibility that promotions were creating structural holes. The researchers removed from the analyses all ties formed after the promotions were achieved. The analyses revealed a complex picture of the effects of structural holes on mobility. Briefly, the effect of having a network rich in structural holes depended on the type of network being studied. For the information network (composed of individuals whom ego relied on for work-related information and advice), managers embedded in large, sparsely connected structures tended to be promoted, a result consistent with the structural-holes perspective. However, for the 'buy- in' network (composed of those individuals whom ego considered essential for getting ego's work done), managers embedded in small, dense networks tended to get promoted (Podolny and Baron, 1997).

More recent work (building on Brass, 1985) has emphasized that actors who bridge across structural holes tend to have high *betweenness centrality* in the social network, in the sense of being go-betweens for those actors not directly connected to each other. In Figure 2.7 (on p. 31), if we assume that all connections are reciprocated, the actor with the highest betweenness centrality is Gery, because he links two different parts of the network together. A recent study showed that individuals with high betweenness centrality in the friendship network in the organization tended to achieve higher performance ratings from supervisors (Mehra et al., 2001). Thus, *centrality* in social networks is implicit in any discussion of social capital or structural holes. There are different ways in which actors can be central. An actor can be popular, in the sense of receiving lots of friendship nominations, and thereby have high *indegree centrality*. In Figure 2.7, both Pam and Steve receive five nominations each, and therefore have the highest indegree centrality of all the actors in the network. Another actor may be central in the sense of having direct and indirect ties to very popular individuals, a type of centrality discussed by Bonacich (1987), and sometimes referred to as *eigenvector centrality* (see Mehra et al., 1998, for an example). In Figure 2.7, Holly has the highest eigenvector centrality because she has ties to popular individuals such as Pam and Don, who in turn have ties to other popular individuals such as Pauline and Michael. An actor may be able to reach lots of people in the network either directly (i.e., the actor's own friends) or indirectly (friends of friends), and thereby have high *closeness centrality*: the actor is close to a large number of other actors in the network. In Figure 2.7, Holly also has the highest closeness centrality of any actor. Although these different measures tend to be highly correlated with each other, they represent quite different conceptions of centrality. (See Davis and Mizuhi, 1999 for three different conceptualizations of centrality in the intercorporate network). Sometimes it may be necessary to control for one type of centrality in order to study the effects of another type. For example, popular actors (those with high indegree centrality) also tend, by virtue of their large numbers of contacts, to have high betweenness centrality. It may be necessary to control for indegree centrality in order to study the effects of betweenness centrality (see the argument in Mehra et al., 2001).

Network Level Concepts

Already in trying to orient the reader towards social network ideas, we have had to use a variety of terms that characterize organizations from a network perspective. The network characteristics of organizations include density, centralization, reachability and balance. These terms help to differentiate different networks in the same organizational unit, or to contrast networks across organizational units.

The *density* of a network is a measure of how many connections there are between actors compared to the maximum possible number of connections that could exist between actors: the higher the proportion, the more dense the network. For example, the density of the instrumental relationship network in an African factory (illustrated in Figure 2.1) is .07, meaning that only 7 per cent of all the possible relationships between people in the factory were established. Density increased to 10 per cent seven months later, as illustrated in Figure 2.2. Comparing densities across different networks is only possible if the networks

FIGURE 2.7

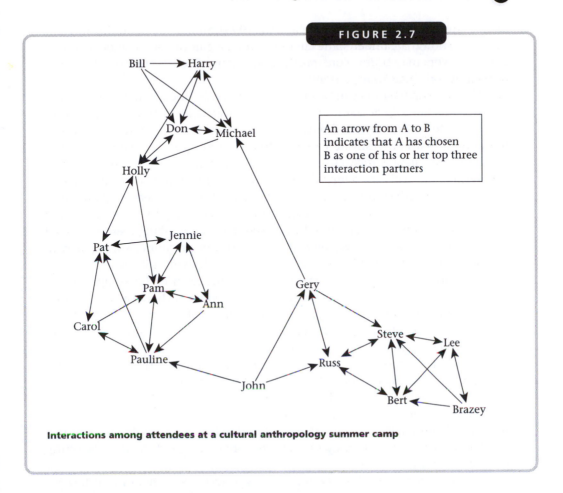

An arrow from A to B indicates that A has chosen B as one of his or her top three interaction partners

Interactions among attendees at a cultural anthropology summer camp

are of approximately the same size. According to the 'law of family interaction' (Bossard, 1945), as the number of actors in a network increases, the number of possible relations between actors increases disproportionately. Thus as the group increases from four to eight members, the number of possible relations increases from six to 28.

Despite the popularity of density as a concept, its use in organizational network research has tended to be reduced to that of a control variable (e.g., Krackhardt and Kilduff, 1999). However, network density can have some counter-intuitive effects on outcomes. For example, a study of the networks of mental health agencies operating in three cities showed that the city with the lowest network-wide density of ties among agencies had the highest effectiveness, whereas the city with the highest density of ties among its agencies had the lowest effectiveness (Provan and Sebastian, 1998). Similarly counter-intuitive is the suggestion that, under some circumstances, a pair of actors embedded in a dense network may be less constrained than a pair of actors embedded in a less dense network (Krackhardt, 1999).

The *centralization* of a network can also provide unexpected insights into network functioning. As mentioned earlier in this chapter, this concept refers to the degree to which the network is centralized around one or a few actors. The researcher can also investigate whether these central actors are themselves clustered together in a structural centre, or whether there are multiple centres throughout the network. Organizations with highly centralized informal networks may tend to be more mechanistic in their functioning, whereas organizations with multiple centres may be more organic (Shrader et al., 1989). A pioneering study of the effects of structural holes showed that high-ranking men embedded in centralized social networks tended to gain slower promotions compared to colleagues embedded in relatively flat networks (Burt, 1992: 158–9).

Networks can also be characterized as to whether they have high or low *reachability*. High-reachability networks are more efficient than low-reachability networks in the sense that messages can reach more of the people through the same number of intermediaries. For example, if in organization A, each individual contacts friends and friends of friends, and through this two-step process all of the people in the organization are contacted, then A has higher reachability than organization B in which the same two-step process reaches only 50 per cent of the people. Mitchell (1969: 16–17) proposed to measure reachability as the average number of people reached per person over all possible steps. In high-reachability networks (compared to low-reachability ones), norms and values may diffuse rapidly to many people with low distortion, ensuring more conformism.

One important question about networks concerns whether or not they are highly structured. The degree of structuring can be assessed in part by measures of *balance* that comprise both reciprocity and transitivity. A network with a high degree of reciprocity is one in which ties between two people tend to be symmetric: if A likes B, then B also likes A. Networks with high transitivity are ones in which ties between three people tend to be complete: if A likes B, and A also likes C, then B and C also like each other. Networks with low reciprocity may be hierarchical, with some stars receiving many nominations that they do not reciprocate. Networks with low transitivity may be less cliquish than those with high transitivity.

Tie-level Concepts

Researchers often discuss the *strength* of an interpersonal tie, defined as a 'combination of the amount of time, the emotional intensity, the intimacy (mutual confiding), and the reciprocal services which characterize the tie' (Granovetter,

1973: 1361). Tie strength ranges from weak (defined in one study as characterizing relationships that are 'infrequent and distant' – see Hansen, 1999: 84) to strong (defined in another study as characterizing relationships that are frequent, long-lasting and affect-laden – see Krackhardt, 1992: 218–19). According to the weak-tie hypothesis, more diverse information is likely to derive from weak than from strong ties (Granovetter, 1973). However, recent research suggests that certain types of strong ties may facilitate the transmission of complex knowledge (Hansen, 1999).

We've already discussed *reciprocity* as one of the characteristics of the whole network, but it is also an important characteristic of each tie between individual actors. Ties can be either symmetric (i.e., reciprocated) or asymmetric (i.e., non-reciprocated). As we will see later in the book, asymmetric ties in some types of relationship (such as friendship) can result in a pressure towards re-establishing symmetry through either breaking the tie or eliciting a stronger response from the non-reciprocating partner. In some types of relations, asymmetry may be the norm. For example, influence relations are typically thought of as asymmetric (De Soto, 1960).

Multiplexity is the extent to which a link between two actors serves a 'multiplicity of interests' (Barnes, 1979: 412). For example, two individuals have a multiplex relationship if they are friends and are also work partners. The term 'multiplex' was coined by one of the Manchester-trained anthropologists in a discussion of judicial affairs among the Barotse of what was then Northern Rhodesia (Gluckman, 1967: 19–20). The multiplexity concept allows the researcher to give a value to each tie based on the number of interests that the tie represents. The link between actors B and C, who are friends, workmates and officemates, would receive a higher tie value in a graph than a link between C and D who are just officemates. There is a sense, then, in which more multiplex relations are considered to have higher tie strength. But multiplexity also represents the extent to which two people are bound to each other in different social arenas. If John and Michael interact as colleagues in the office, friends on the weekend, and teammates on the firm's basketball team, then there are three social circles in which they meet each other. For an individual to break part of a multiplex tie might involve the individual in difficulties with the other parts of the tie. For example, for John to break the friendship bond with Michael might make relations in the office and on the basketball team strained.

SUMMARY

In this chapter we presented an overview of the wide range of methods and motivations that comprise the network approach. We described the origins of the social network perspective, and showed how social network research offers a distinctive focus on social relations, the linking of micro and macro levels, and the integration of qualitative, quantitative and graphical data. We discussed orienting concepts such as social capital, embeddedness, network centrality and structural holes that are of particular interest to management and organizational scholars. With a good understanding of concepts and methods, readers are ready to enjoy the debates and controversies presented in the following chapters. In the next chapter we tackle the debate around what constitutes network theory, a debate of crucial importance to organizational researchers.

RECOMMENDED FURTHER READING

Leinhardt, S. (ed.). 1977. *Social networks: A developing paradigm.* New York: Academic Press.
A collection of classic articles, reproduced exactly as they were originally published, including pieces by Fritz Heider, James Davis, François Lorrain and Harrison White, Jeffrey Travers and Stanley Milgram, Elizabeth Bott, Mark Granovetter, and Frank Harary. The topics covered include attitude formation, small world problem, weak ties, structural equivalence, interorganizational networks, and graph theory.

Nohria, N. and Eccles, R.G. (eds). 1992. *Networks and organizations: Structure, form and action.* Boston, MA: Harvard Business School Press.
This collection offers a broad cross-sectional summary of work accomplished in the previous twenty years, with valuable excerpts of work by Ronald S. Burt, and Mark Granovetter among contributions by other leading contemporary organizational social network researchers.

Scott, J. 2000. *Social network analysis: A handbook.* 2nd edn. Newbury Park, CA: Sage.
This is the most lucid guide to network methods currently available, and is essential reading for everyone contemplating research.

Wasserman, S. and Faust, K. 1994. *Social network analysis: Methods and application.* New York: Cambridge University Press.
A comprehensive guide to social network methods, this book is an excellent companion to all network researchers. It serves as a reference book to be consulted in search of definitions and explanations of network research terms and procedures.

3 Is There Social Network Theory? A Critical Examination of Theoretical Foundations

One of the perennial questions that social network researchers argue over is whether the network approach is a collection of methods, or whether it represents a distinctive theoretical perspective. For many people, the social network field is a collection of methods, providing algorithms for operationalizing a range of important concepts such as centrality, structural equivalence, cliques, and so on. As fascinating and as useful as these methods are, it is hard to argue that they constitute a theory. Certainly the social network field is rich with analytical tools ranging from algorithms that simulate various types of organizational outcome to suites of software programs that allow even beginners to produce sophisticated analyses. For this reason influential researchers such as John Scott (2000: 37) argue that social network analysis is an 'orientation towards the social world that inheres in a particular set of *methods*. It is not a specific body of formal or substantive social theory.' But others have claimed to detect in the social network approach 'a theory of social structures' (Degenne and Forse, 1999: 12) that approaches the elusive Kuhnian ideal of a mature paradigm (Hummon and Carley, 1993).

The debate among social network researchers resounds also in the corridors and chambers where organizational social network researchers gather. Everyone seems to agree that the network approach has useful concepts and analytical methods for exploring predictions of other theories such as population ecology (e.g., Burt, 1992: 208–27). But every attempt to produce organizational network theory tends to be greeted with the disparaging argument that there is nothing particularly distinctive to a network approach here and that a good network theory of organization is still wanted (see Salancik, 1995).

WHAT IS A THEORY?

We should begin by asking ourselves: What constitutes a theory? Is it a set of causally linked concepts concerning some aspects of the world from which one derives falisifiable hypotheses? Or is a theory 'an abstract, symbolic representation of, and explanation of, social reality' (Adams and Sydie, 2001: 4)? Is a theory judged on the basis of its predictive validity or on the basis of its descriptive validity? These questions relate to major debates in the philosophy of science. We can not settle those debates here, but we can suggest what might be some issues that any social network theory, whether predictive or descriptive, whether concerned solely with organizations or not, might be expected to achieve.

Any social network theory has to address issues germane to social networks. That much seems obvious. What are some of these issues? Irrespective of whether we are discussing individuals or organizations, the issues of tie formation, evolution and dissolution are within the realm of any putative social network theory. The concept of a tie between two actors is perhaps the most basic concept in social networks, and therefore must be addressed in any theory. Further, we expect any such theory to inform us concerning the origins and outcomes of actors' structural positions in networks. By structural position we mean centrality, for example. Note that in addressing questions of origins and outcomes, we necessarily stray away from purely network topics to include a whole range of concepts (demographic, economic, etc.) that might affect or result from actors' network positions.

Do descriptions of social network structure count as theory? To the extent that some enduring features of social network structure are habitually discovered in specific networks, then there is a basis for theorizing concerning the types of network structure, their causes and consequences. But representations of specific networks disconnected from any claims to generalizability appear to offer little basis for prediction and little help to those seeking to understand the enduring nature of social networks.

Does a collection of related concepts constitute a theory? If we throw together such important ideas as *embeddedness, social capital, structural holes* and so on, does the sheer brilliance of insights constitute a theory? It is possible that there is an underlying logic that relates the concepts to each other, that explains, for example, how weak ties contribute to or detract from embeddedness, thus affecting social capital. Efforts at such theorizing are likely to be many, given the level of interest in such concepts. But interest in the social sciences for grand theorizing that links vaguely defined concepts in loose causal schemes has been on the wane at least since Merton's (1957) call for theories of the middle range. We do not attempt to create a Rube Goldberg theory of network concepts.

EXISTING THEORY DEVELOPMENT ON SOCIAL NETWORKS

As we look over the existing work in social networks, we find three categories of research and thinking. First, the social network field is characterized by *imported theories*, that is, theories borrowed from other disciplines, including mathematics and social psychology. From mathematics, graph theoretical ideas have provided one continuing basis for social network research. From social psychology, imports have included balance theory and social comparison theory — these have been colonized, changed and extended by network researchers. Borrowed theories have been reconfigured to such an extent that a distinctive network agenda has begun to emerge. Thus, we examine in detail the contributions of these borrowed theories for emergent social network approaches to organizations.

Second, there are at least two claimants to the title of *home-grown or indigenous social network theories*: (1) Heterophily theory which includes the concepts of the strength of weak ties and structural holes, and makes predictions concerning how actors' ties outside closed social circles can access diverse knowledge and other resources; (2) Structural role theory which includes the concepts of structural equivalence, structural cohesion and role equivalence, and makes predictions concerning how actors in networks influence each others' attitudes and behaviours. We examine further how these two indigenous approaches overlap in terms of concepts and predictions, and the extent to which they form a platform from which new indigenous theory can be developed.

Third, there is considerable *exportation* of network ideas into existing organizational theories. Researchers take existing organization theories, critique them from a social network perspective, and synthesize them with social network concepts and approaches. There is excellent work from a resource dependence perspective investigating decisions concerning the choice of banking partners (Baker, 1990). Others have built bridges between structural-hole concepts and population ecology (e.g., Burt, 1992) and between the weak-tie hypothesis and contingency theory (e.g., Hansen, 1999). Some of the most interesting social network research critiques or modifies the transaction costs approach in the process of enlarging the domain of social network ideas (e.g., Granovetter, 1985; Uzzi, 1996). We explore further the potential for more critical engagement between organization theory and social network concepts.

We consider here how social network theory has been built from mathematical foundations, how borrowings from balance theory and social comparison theory have facilitated distinctive theoretical social network research, how indigenous work in heterophily and structural-hole role theory offer promising research opportunities, and conclude with a brief review of the possibilities apparent to us in developing a critical synthesis of social network concepts and existing organization theories. Whereas the borrowed theories we discuss relate mainly to the micro-level interactions of individuals, the indigenous theories hold promise of facilitating research at both micro and macro levels.

IMPORTED THEORIES: BORROWINGS FROM OTHER DISCIPLINES

Borrowings from Mathematics

Social network analysis derives many of its concepts from graph theory. Points and lines (as understood in graph theory) conveniently represent actors and their ties (as understood in social network analysis), directed graphs (with one or two way arrows) are used to represent the degree of reciprocation between actors, and so on (see Harary et al., 1965, for an introduction to graph theory). We consider a recent example of how ideas from graph theory have been adapted for use in the arena of organizational social networks.

Can graph theory help us understand the extent to which networks reflect divided social systems, mechanistic organization, organizational effectiveness, and ease of resolving conflicts? The answer is yes, according to recent work that examines four graph-theoretic aspects of informal organization (Krackhardt, 1994). The first aspect is *degree of connectedness*, which refers to the extent to which the actors are able to connect to each other through the network. If there is no path from one actor to the other actor, then the two actors are disconnected.

As Figure 3.1 shows, a social system (as represented by a graph) can exhibit differing degrees of connectedness. The right-hand digraph (so named because

FIGURE 3.1

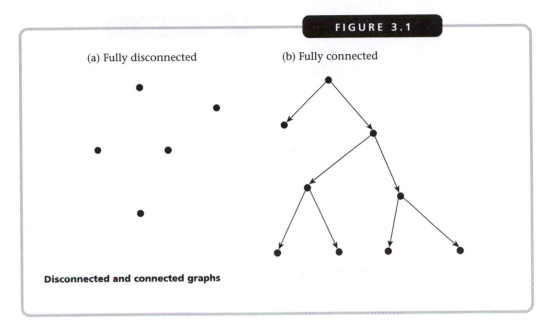

(a) Fully disconnected   (b) Fully connected

Disconnected and connected graphs

of the arrows indicating the direction of the social ties) illustrates a system in which all actors can reach all other actors, whereas the left-hand graph illustrates a system in which no actor can reach any other actor. Notice that, according to graph theory, each point in Figure 3.1(b) can reach every other point in the underlying graph in which the direction of the arrows is ignored. It is in this sense that Figure 3.1(b) is considered to be a digraph that is connected (Krackhardt, 1994: 91–3).

Disconnectedness indicates division in the social system. A severely disconnected communication network may impair the organization's ability to engage its members in consultation. Similarly, increasing connectedness in an organizational system may signal increased resource-sharing and collaboration (Powell et al., 1996: 143).

The second aspect is *graph hierarchy*. This refers to the extent to which the informal organization is hierarchical, with relations of authority proceeding in a single direction from those with more status to those with less. The greater the hierarchy, the more the informal network resembles an organizational chart of a status-conscious mechanistic organization. Figure 3.1(b) is fully hierarchical, with influence flowing from the top down. Research has shown that people expect influence relations to be hierarchical, and have difficulty learning social networks in which influence relations violate the kind of one-way direction of influence illustrated in Figure 3.1(b) (De Soto, 1960). For example, people have difficulty learning the social structure depicted in Figure 3.2 because it systematically violates our notions of a 'pecking order'.

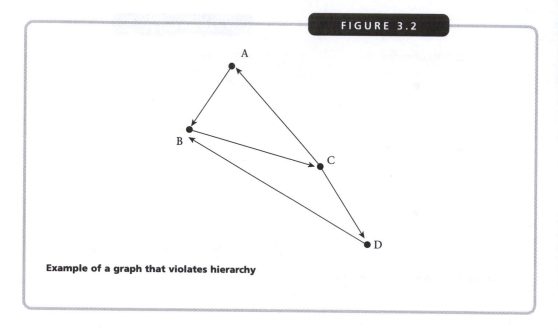

FIGURE 3.2

Example of a graph that violates hierarchy

The third aspect is *graph efficiency* which measures the degree to which the number of links in the network approaches the minimum necessary to prevent the network fragmenting into two separate parts. To the extent that efficiency is violated, the network has redundant links that 'take time and resources to maintain' (Krackhardt, 1994: 98). A perfectly efficient network is fragile in the sense of being 'vulnerable to the arbitrary deletion of a link' through attrition (Krackhardt, 1994: 99). Krackhardt speculates that there may be a curvilinear relationship between graph efficiency and organizational effectiveness, with effectiveness first rising with increasing efficiency and then falling as the network becomes increasingly bare bones.

Figure 3.1(b) is perfectly efficient in the sense that the number of links between the actors is precisely one fewer than the number of actors: there are no redundant links. If one link is removed for any reason (one individual stops giving advice to another), then the organizational network becomes disconnected. A clique (in which all actors are connected to all other actors) represents the maximum inefficiency, in which a lot of time may be spent in networking activity, with each employee expected to connect to everyone else.

The fourth graph-theoretic aspect that might offer theoretical insight into the functioning of organizational social networks is *least upper boundedness*. This concerns the extent to which each pair of actors has access to a third person (the 'upper bound'), to whom they both defer. Figure 3.1(b) illustrates an organization fully consistent with this 'unity-of-command' principle, whereas

FIGURE 3.3

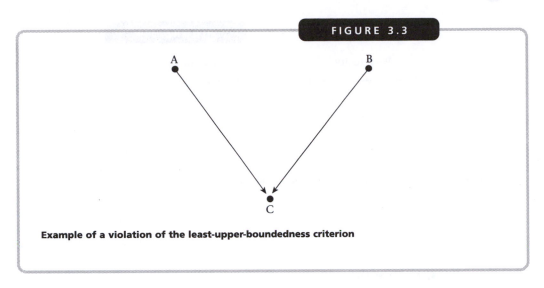

Example of a violation of the least-upper-boundedness criterion

Figure 3.3 shows a situation where pair A and B have no common superior, and person C suffers from influence from two 'bosses'. In networks in which few of the pairs have a least-upper-bound actor to appeal to, conflict may be difficult to resolve.

Krackhardt's (1994) success in mapping graph theory on to organizational phenomena is unusual, and should spur other efforts to find isomorphism between the purely mathematical relations inherent in graphs and the structures of relations evident in organizational life. Going beyond graph theory is also a possibility given the success of computational approaches in simulating predictable features of network relations within and between organizations (e.g., Carley and Prietula, 1994).

Borrowings from Social Psychology

We organize our review of the large number of theoretical insights borrowed from social psychology under the general headings of balance theory and social comparison theory. Balance theory, to the extent that it concerns individuals' tendencies to promote connections between their friends, naturally encompasses discussion of cliques, clique overlaps, and the special case of friendship dyads embedded within three-person friendship cliques (known as Simmelian triads). Social comparison theory addresses people's tendencies, when faced with important evaluation or decision tasks, to compare themselves with similar others. This theory offers predictions concerning the network connections that people forge, and the effects of these connections on attitudes and behaviours.

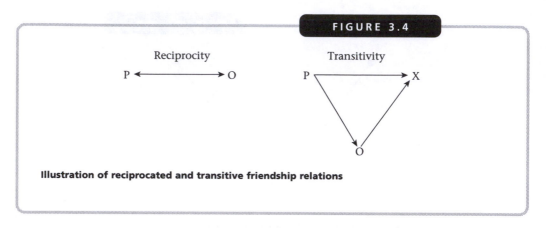

FIGURE 3.4

Reciprocity

Transitivity

Illustration of reciprocated and transitive friendship relations

Balance Theory

Balance theory was developed as a theory of cognitive consistency (Heider, 1958), but has been developed into a wide-ranging framework for understanding interpersonal influence. The key breakthrough was the translation of Heider's concepts into graph-theoretic terms (Cartwright and Harary, 1956) and the subsequent extension of balance theory from cognitive processes to structural processes (see Davis, 1963, for a summary).

Interpersonal balance theory starts with some simple postulates concerning people's preferences. The theory is usually stated in terms of persons P and O and their attitudes towards an object (or third person) X. These ideas can be summarized in non-technical language as follows (see Davis, 1963, for a graph-theoretic treatment).

I. People prefer balanced relationships; for example, they prefer their friendships to be reciprocated, and for their friends to be friends of each other. More precisely, if P is friends with O, then there is pressure on O to be friends with P (reciprocity). If P is friends with O and O is friends with X, then there is pressure on P to be friends with X also (transitivity). A reciprocated friendship tie is illustrated in Figure 3.4, as is a transitive friendship triad. Balance refers to these two aspects of social ties: reciprocity and transitivity.

II. Related to the first point, people prefer to interact with others, with whom they share strong attachments to one or more shared characteristics. These characteristics could be such salient factors as ethnicity and gender. More precisely, the likelihood that P and O will interact increases to the extent that P and O both have a strong attachment to X.

III. To the extent that people are involved in unbalanced relationships, they suffer feelings of discomfort. Unbalance can result from unrequited friendship, for example. Or an individual who has a strong attachment to a particular demographic identity may experience discomfort when confronted with a friend's indifference or hostility towards that identity. Thus, if P is friends with O but O is not friends with P, then P will suffer discomfort. Similarly, if P and O are friends and P has a strong positive regard for X whereas O is indifferent to X, then P will suffer discomfort.

IV. People will act to change unbalanced relationships into balanced ones. Balance can be re-established by either changing other people's attitudes or breaking off relationships. Thus, if P is friends with O but O is not friends with P, P can either try harder to elicit friendship tokens from O or P can break off the friendship tie to O in order to establish balance.

Preferences for balanced relationships

Balance theory focuses attention on the interpersonal structures of organizations and in particular on the ways in which organizations split into different tightly-knit groups, or cliques. One of the most interesting derivations from balance theory propositions is that, if the relationships in an organization are completely balanced, then the organization can be divided into two groups such that all the ties within each group are positive and all the ties between groups are negative (Cartwright and Harary, 1956). Balance theory has many other surprising implications for organizational behaviour, such as the following: the existence of complicated group structures (interlocking groups formed around many dimensions) enhances the unity of the organization 'because for any given person there are fewer others who are socially identical or socially disparate' (Davis, 1963: 454); the existence of sub-groups prevents group fragmentation 'by making less probable the development of large, cohesive cliques set totally apart from the rest of the group' (Davis, 1963, 454); larger groups afford more possibilities for clique membership because of the greater probability 'that a person with a particular combination of characteristics can find sufficient others to form a clique' (Davis, 1963: 455); and marginal members – those with a tie to more than one group – are likely to be the transmitters of innovation from one group to another (Davis, 1963: 456).

Fortunately, relationships in most organizational settings do not approach the extreme case of polarization into two opposed factions. In a review of a huge data bank of 1,000 networks, balance was most closely approximated in networks of junior high school students. Davis (1979: 60), in his review of this research, comments that, 'If I were to choose a group to join, the last thing in the world I'd like would be one divided into tight cliques and arranged in an iron pecking order of popularity.'

Balance theory is useful not just at the interpersonal level in organizations, but also for understanding tie formation at the interorganizational level. Ethnographic research on the formation of trading relationships between firms conclusively demonstrates the importance of personal contacts involving friendship as one basis for tie formation. The process of building the trust necessary for successful interorganizational collaboration involves reciprocity and transitivity. As Larson (1992: 87) wrote: 'The building process for the network organization relied heavily on trust and the development of reciprocity norms during a trial period.' Managers even used the term 'balance' to describe the importance of reciprocity as a structural component of alliance formation, as in this quote from an executive: 'It is like a balance, a scale – in return for commitment on their part we say we are committed to you and we prove it. So it's a *quid pro quo*. It's a balanced relationship that says you make investments, we make investments; you take risks, we take risks; you perform, we perform' (quoted in Larson, 1992: 89). As one actor built trust with two other actors in the industry, processes of transitivity tended to promote the dense structuring of organizational fields. As Uzzi (1996: 679) discussed in his investigation of tie formation in the New York garment industry: 'One actor with an embedded tie to each of two unconnected actors acts as their go-between by using her common link to establish trustworthiness between them.' Thus, organizational representatives tended to bring exchange partners together, creating denser links between firms in the industry (see Powell et al., 1996).

Balance theory indicates that people (within organizations and as representatives of organizations) will tend to form cliques as a by-product of their preference for balanced relationships. Cliques are therefore an inevitable structural component of organizations from a balance theory perspective. Given the extent to which these important structural components have been neglected in organizational research, it is worth reviewing the basic techniques, definitions and types of theory-driven research on cliques in organizational settings.

Cliques

What is a clique? We will offer a formal definition shortly, but here is one attempt at an intuitive definition compatible with balance theory: 'A subset of group members whose average liking for each other is greater than their average liking for the other members [in the group] is a clique' (Davis, 1963: 451). One of the most famous examples of clique analysis in the organizational literature concerned the 14 members of the bank wiring room whose game-playing network we showcase in the example in the Appendix from data collected by Roethlisberger and Dickson (1939). The data have been re-examined by many others, most famously by George Homans (1950). The Hawthorne researchers found that the wiremen, soldermen and inspectors formed themselves into two groups: 'Whether the investigators looked at games, job trading, quarrels over windows, or friendships and antagonisms, two groups seemed to stand out. One of these groups was located toward the front of the room, the other toward the back. "The

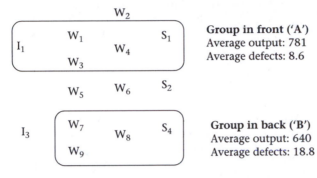

FIGURE 3.5

W = Wiremen, S = Soldermen, I = Inspectors

Group in front ('A')
Average output: 781
Average defects: 8.6

Group in back ('B')
Average output: 640
Average defects: 18.8

Two groups in the bank wiring room of the Hawthorne works

group in front" and "the group in back" were common terms of designation among the workmen themselves' (Roethlisberger and Dickson, 1939: 508).

The groups (named A and B by the researchers) were spatially organized and cut across occupational specialities. Figure 3.5 shows the membership of the two groups: solid lines contain those members that the researchers could definitely place within a group. The members of group A regarded themselves as superior to group B (Roethlisberger and Dickson, 1939: 510). This attitude of superiority showed up in many different ways. Compared to group B members, members of group A tended to trade jobs less, refrain from controversies about opening windows, engage in games of chance rather than rough-housing, purchase small quantities of chocolate candy rather than larger quantities of less expensive candy, and prefer verbal arguments over horseplay.

Group membership affected not only these voluntary activities, but also the performance of the workers. The members of group A conformed in all respects to the room-wide informal code of conduct that the workers had developed to monitor their own productivity. This code consisted of the following mandates: (1) you should not turn out too much work; (2) you should not turn out too little work; (3) you should not 'squeal' to the supervisor about the behaviour of an associate; (4) you should not act officious, even if you are an inspector. Members of group B were adamant in their support of all these rules except rule 2. A comparison of the average productivity of the members of the two groups shows that the wiremen in A outperformed their colleagues in B by producing more connections per hour and less defects per 100,000 connections.

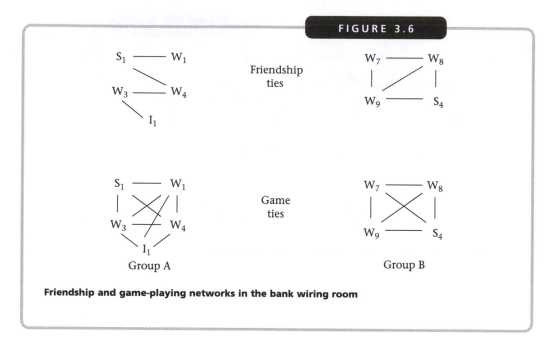

FIGURE 3.6

Friendship and game-playing networks in the bank wiring room

Visual inspection of Figure 3.6, which shows friendship and game-playing relations in the bank wiring room, gives an immediate sense that there are indeed two distinct groups. But, are these groups cliques? In network analysis (borrowing from graph theory), the term 'clique' has been formally defined as follows: *For a clique to exist, all the actors must be directly connected to each other; and all the actors must have no direct common link to any other actor.* By convention, the term 'clique' is restricted to groups of three or more actors so that mutual dyads are not considered to be cliques (Wasserman and Faust, 1994: 254). In the language of graph theory, a clique is a maximal complete subgraph (Luce and Perry, 1949). Figure 3.6 shows that, by this strict definition, only B can be considered a clique: every member of B engaged in games with every other member. Note that the friendship relations in B do not comprise a clique in this strict sense, because of the absence of a tie between W7 and S4.

To find a set of actors that satisfies this strict definition of a clique is rare, so network analysts have offered alternative definitions that help identify the structure of informal groups. N-cliques are groups of actors who can all reach each other through a maximum of n links. Thus, the games network for group A in Figure 3.6 is a 5-member 2-clique because each of the 5 members can reach every other member directly (1 link) or indirectly through a third party (2 links). Similarly, the friendship network for clique B is a 4-member 2-clique.

The k-plex approach to clique identification also relaxes the strict definition of a clique. A set of n actors is considered to be a k-plex if each actor is connected to at least n-k actors. If $k = 2$, for example, then the four members of the friendship network of group B in Figure 3.6 is a 2-plex because each actor is linked to at least n-2 other actors. (See Scott, 2000: 117–20; and Wasserman and Faust, 1994: 249–90, for further discussion of graph theory and cliques.)

Clique overlap

A rare study that used the strict definition of a clique as a maximal complete sub-graph examined the networks of mental health agencies of similar size in three US cities. The most effective pattern of health care was provided in the city with the least number of cliques, but the highest clique overlap. Clique overlap referred to the extent to which members of a clique interacted with members of other cliques. Thus, clique overlap was a measure of mental health system integration. Particularly important was the extent of clique multiplexity, defined as the extent to which cliques based on one type of relationship (the referral network) overlapped with cliques based on another type of relationship (the case coordination network). Figure 3.7(a) illustrates how members of a clique can have overlapping multiplex relationships (as indicated by the existence of both full and dashed lines) or uniplex relations as shown in Figure 3.7(b). As the authors stated: 'In a system with high clique overlap, many clique members would also be members of other cliques, thus providing a highly integrated core of provider agencies spanning multiple cliques' (Provan and Sebastian, 1998: 458). It was the intensive integration through network cliques that determined network effectiveness, whereas the degree of integration across the full network was negatively related to effectiveness: The most effective network had the lowest network-wide integration (as measured by the density of links among agencies) whereas the least effective network had the highest network-wide integration. The Provan and Sebastian research indicates the extent to which clique overlap can be an important network variable related to outcomes at the network level of analysis.

Simmelian ties

At the individual level of analysis, the question of membership in overlapping cliques also has theoretical significance. What happens when two people in an organization who are friends both belong to one or more of the same cliques? Their friendship tie is embedded in a social context of norms and values that limits the degree to which the pair of individuals can create their own norms and values. A dyadic tie between two people who both belong to the same clique has been called a Simmelian tie. (See Figure 3.8 for an illustration.) Recent work (Krackhardt, 1998, 1999) has focused on these kinds of embedded dyadic relationship, building from the discussion initiated by Georg Simmel, the German sociologist. Simmel discussed how three-person cliques (triads) differed from two-person relationships (dyads). Triads tend to suppress individual interests, reduce individual power and moderate conflict (see the discussion in Krackhardt, 1999: 185). Individual interests within a triad can be outvoted by a coalition of the other two members on any issue. Further, whereas any

FIGURE 3.7

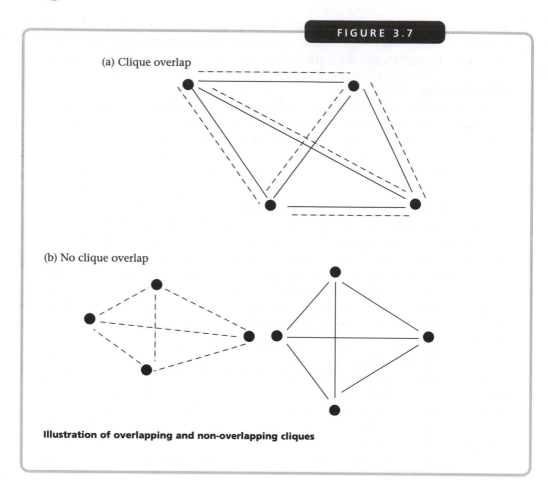

(a) Clique overlap

(b) No clique overlap

Illustration of overlapping and non-overlapping cliques

individual can threaten to break up a dyadic relation by considering withdrawal, such threats are less powerful in triads given that there will always be two people left to carry on. Conflict in triads between two people can be moderated and repaired by the intervention of the third person.

Krackhardt (1999) defined a Simmelian tie as a connection between two people that is embedded in a clique. He argued that dyads embedded in cliques are more constrained in their attitudes and behaviour than dyads independent of cliques. Some dyads are embedded in many cliques and therefore are subject to the norms of all of these cliques. This embeddedness considerably limits the freedom of the two individual members of the dyad. A partial test of the idea that Simmelian-tied dyads were more constrained than dyads in general examined the degree of consensus between individuals connected by dyadic ties in three organizations. The results showed that for the advice and friendship networks, individuals in Simmelian-tied dyads (compared to dyads in general)

FIGURE 3.8

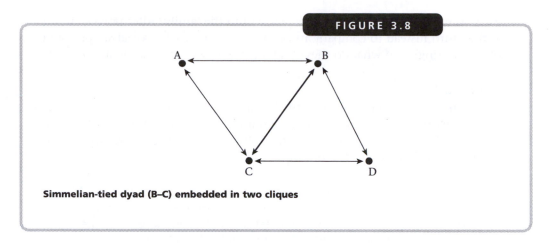

Simmelian-tied dyad (B–C) embedded in two cliques

tended to exhibit more consensus concerning the structure of organizational social worlds (Krackhardt and Kilduff, 2002). The individual members of these Simmelian-tied dyads tended to perceive the social world more similarly than individuals in dyads that were not embedded in cliques.

Social Comparison Theory

Balance theory concerns itself with the ways in which people arrange their existing relationships to reduce feelings of imbalance. But why do people choose to interact with certain others in the first place? One important principle that underlies much social network research is that people prefer to interact with others who are similar to themselves in important and salient respects. According to Festinger's (1954) formulation of social comparison theory, (a) human beings learn about themselves by comparing themselves to others; (b) people choose similar others with whom to compare; and (c) social comparisons will have strong effects on attitudes and opinions when no objective non-social basis of comparison is available and when the opinion is very important to the individual (see Goethals and Darley, 1987, for a review of social comparison research).

From a social comparison perspective, we are drawn into friendships with similar others in order to be able to evaluate our opinions and abilities. We seek out people in the same ability ranges as ourselves in order to determine more precisely our own levels of skill. Pressure to adopt opinions, to acquire skills or to strive for outcomes such as promotions comes from our social comparisons with those whom we regard as similar to us.

The question of who is the social comparison other has been investigated in many different contexts, including that of relations between the sexes. When do husbands and wives see each other as comparison others and therefore come to resemble each other in the roles they play within the family? Alternatively, when do they turn instead to companions of their own gender for social support and role mentoring? And what do these findings mean for organizational research?

Bott hypothesis

One of the earliest and most influential examinations of the sex segregation of social networks was conducted among a sample of married couples in London. On the basis of extensive interviews the following hypothesis was deduced as a tentative explanation of the findings:

> The degree of segregation in the role-relationship of husband and wife varies directly with the connectedness of the family's social network. The more connected the network, the greater the degree of segregation between the roles of husband and wife. The less connected the network, the smaller the degree of segregation between the roles of husband and wife. (Bott, 1957: 60)

The basic idea elaborated by Bott was that roles that husbands and wives played within the marriage depended on the network of relationships that surrounded the married pair. Married couples embedded in sparse networks characterized by relatively few ties between people tended to be thrown on each others' resources and to develop patterns of helping that reduced major differences in role relationships. Thus, the husband would tend to help with the children, the housework and the shopping. The members of the dyad A–B in Figure 3.9(a) each have three (different) connections to others, but there are no ties between the dyad's connections. A has her three connections and B has his three connections. The dyad is embedded in a loosely-knit network of ties.

Married couples embedded in closely-knit networks (illustrated in Figure 3.9(b) tended to be quite different. The woman tended to have female relatives and female neighbours available to help with work that was considered typically female in nature, whereas the man tended to have male friends available for typically male recreational pursuits.

Bott's key insight represents perhaps the first data-inspired recognition that dyadic relationships are shaped in important ways by the larger context of social relationships surrounding the dyad. Individuals occupy positions in informal social networks and bring influences from these networks to bear on their dyadic interactions. Her inductions were later supported with longitudinal analyses on a random sample of working-class wives in New Haven, Connecticut. Briefly, the researchers found that wives whose social relations were embedded in cliques were more likely to maintain traditional family orientations with their husbands than were wives whose social relations tended to consist of ties to individuals unconnected to each other (Nelson, 1966).

What, one may ask, does any of this have to do with social network relations in formal organizations? There has been little work extending Bott's ideas

FIGURE 3.9

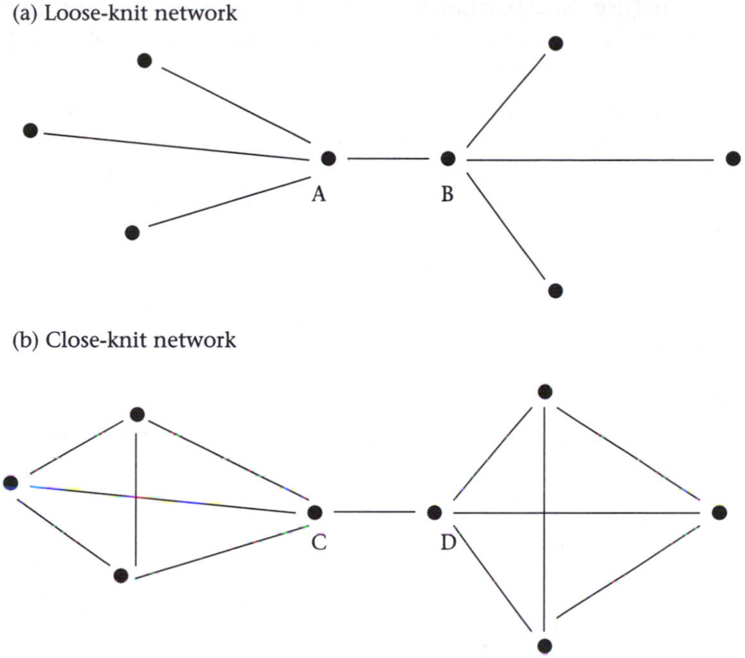

(a) Loose-knit network

(b) Close-knit network

Dyads embedded in loose- and close-knit networks

to relationships within work organizations. Researchers in the area of occupational communities have suggested that night shift workers tend to be cut off from family and extra-family social networks and therefore tend to develop primary ties with each other, developing strong bonds of mutual support with co-workers (Lipset et al., 1956). In the absence of social support from others, such isolated workers may, in general, be likely to develop relatively egalitarian norms of social interaction. Similarly, a dyadic relationship between a supervisor and a subordinate may be more likely to approximate a friendship tie rather than a one-way authority tie to the extent that both supervisor and subordinate are free from the constraints of clique-embeddedness with peers. If a supervisor is embeddeded in a clique with other supervisors, then he or she is more likely to be constrained to uphold supervisory attitudes and behaviour in interactions with subordinates, and less likely to have free time or sociability to spend on building friendship ties with subordinates.

Although researchers on embeddedness at the organizational level have neglected the structural similarity of their work to the pioneering insights of

Bott, there is considerable overlap. Just as the nature of the marriage tie between husband and wife depends on the social ties of each spouse to friends and kin, the nature of a partnership between one firm and another firm is influenced by the kinds of network in which each firm is embedded. For the focal firm, the pattern of embeddedness that promotes continued survival in a competitive market is of the following kind: build strong ties with those alliance partners whose own networks of relationships include a mix of strong ties and arm's length, market-based transacting (Uzzi, 1996). Thus, from the focal firm's perspective, in choosing another firm as a business partner, it is important to consider the embeddedness of that firm in its network of relations. Just as the marriage union of a man and woman is also the union of two sets of families and two sets of other social relations, so the alliance between two companies involves a tie between two sets of business bonds.

Homophily

The principle of homophily underlies many processes of social interaction. The basic idea is simple: people like to associate with others who are similar. Similar others are helpful in evaluating one's ideas and abilities, especially when important consequences are at stake (Festinger, 1954). The bases upon which people can choose similar others are, of course, many. Among the most salient bases of social interaction are demographic factors such as sex, ethnicity, religion and age.

Individuals are likely to belong to many sub-groupings in organizations: a person can simultaneously be white, female, young, Canadian and Catholic, for example, and may find herself drawn to people of each of these different groups for the purposes of social comparison. Each of us exists at the intersection of cross-cutting social circles that define our individuality. As Simmel (1955) pointed out, and as Blau (1984) has formalized, the more affiliations to such groups that an individual has, the more diverse and counteracting the pressures on individuals, and, therefore, the weaker the hold any one group has on its members. More memberships therefore tend to equal more options and more freedom for the individual. How do these pressures work out in an organizational context?

Recent research indicates that the pressure to interact with similar others in organizations may vary according to the relative numbers of similar others there are in different social categories. As predicted by balance theory, organizations are often characterized by segregated networks composed of people similar on some salient and valued variable such as gender, race or ideology. In one newspaper organization characterized by unusually high balance in terms of reciprocated network ties averaging around 80 per cent, men and women tended to form their own networks, with men choosing male partners 75 per cent of the time, whereas women chose females 68 per cent of the time. Brass (1985: 339) summarized this phenomenon as follows: 'There appeared to be two informal, segregated networks operating in the organization.' Women tended to interact with other women, and men with other men. In another organization social relations among 16 members of upper management fragmented into two clique-like groups. Between these two groups there tended to be a far higher percentage of negative feelings than within the groups and a much lower percentage of positive feelings (White, 1961: 197). The two groups had opposing views (amounting to distinctly different ideologies) concerning an issue that was vital for organizational survival: the future of research and development in the organization.

The literature on homophily pressures in organizations shows that, in general, people tend to interact with similar others, and this tendency is particularly marked for relations, such as friendship, that are more expressive than instrumental (Blau, 1977; Ibarra, 1992) and in which, therefore, pressures towards balance are likely to be greatest. The question of which types of similar others people are likely to interact with has been partially answered by considering the distinctiveness of social groups in particular contexts. In a study of social identity and friendship relations, the results showed that the relative rarity of a social category (such as gender or race) promoted members' use of that category as a basis for social identification and friendship formation. Thus, for racial minorities, race was a stronger category for social identification and friendship than gender, whereas for the white majority, gender, not race, was a stronger category (Mehra et al., 1998).

The potential for social psychology to contribute further to the emergence of distinctive social network theory is huge. Indeed, we devote the next chapter to a deeper look at two particularly promising network approaches (cognitive network theory and an emergent personality approach to social structure) that draw heavily from themes covered in this section.

HOME-GROWN NETWORK THEORIES

Heterophily Theory

We have just reviewed research suggesting that people have a strong tendency to cluster together on the basis of shared characteristics for purposes of social comparison and support. It might be supposed, therefore, that informal networks in organizations are in danger of fragmenting into separate groups with little or no contact between them. Indeed, problems of fragmentation are common in organizations. Sometimes employees in a department 'spend all their time talking among themselves and neglect to cultivate relationships with the rest of their colleagues' in other departments. Or, just as troublesome, employees in a department may 'communicate only with members of other groups and not among themselves' (see the discussion in Krackhardt and Hanson, 1993: 110). In either situation, the result is that discrete groups of informally-linked employees form bonds of communication and trust. In the absence of strong ties between these groups, little tacit knowledge or expertise is likely to flow (Hansen, 1999).

Given the strong preferences individuals and other social actors exhibit towards homophily, it may seem strange to suggest that there are circumstances in which the opposite tendency – heterophily – may occur. But heterophily theory has a long history in the social sciences, starting with Simmel's (1950) discussion of the stranger who dwells in the heart of one society yet retains allegiance to a different society. The stranger is a role that is both near and remote from the group within which it is embedded. Those occupying the stranger role can use their distant and proximate connections to broker relations between the groups within which they dwell and the groups with which they maintain distant relations. The stranger, then, is also the trader, one who brings news, new inventions, new intelligence into relatively closed economic groups. The stranger is more mobile than those among whom he or she dwells, tending to have less strong ties of kinship and so on compared to others.

The heterophily perspective therefore suggests that new information and unusual resources tend to flow from relative strangers who may be members of other social organizations, or who may be brokers joining groups that are themselves disconnected. Much of the most exciting recent work in social networks has extended and refined these ideas. We look in some detail at the weak ties and the structural-hole extensions of heterophily theory.

Strength of weak ties

How are organizations knit together if people tend to cluster in homogeneous groups of like-minded employees? One of the most insightful analyses of this situation was offered by Mark Granovetter (1973, 1982) who started with the observation that, from the perspective of balance theory, the likelihood of finding the so-called 'forbidden triad' (Figure 3.10) was low for strong relationships such as friendship.

The O–X link is likely to be completed because of the strain towards balance. But if the relationships in Figure 3.9 are considered weak (e.g., acquaintances rather than friends), then the pressures towards balance are diminished or non-existent. If P knows two people as acquaintances, then P may feel no pressure to bring these people together. The significance of this distinction between strong ties (such as friendship) and weak ties (such as acquaintanceship) lies in the probability that forbidden triads may be embedded in much larger structures.

Consider, for example, Figure 3.11. If P has weak ties of acquaintanceship with X and O, then two important consequences follow: (1) P serves as a 'bridge' for information to flow between cliques Alpha and Beta; and (2) there is no pressure on P to balance the P–O–X triad because these are acquaintanceship relations not friendship relations. Thus, in order for someone in clique Alpha to learn of opportunities or techniques known by people in clique Beta, the knowledge must flow through P. Granovetter (1973) points out that

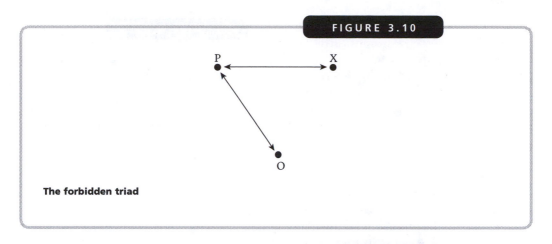

FIGURE 3.10

The forbidden triad

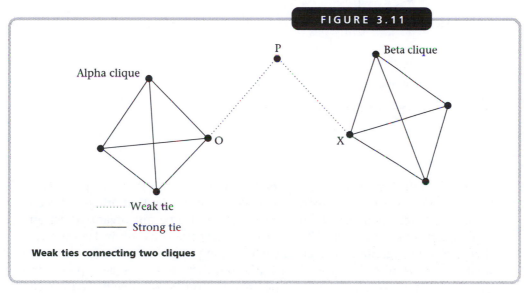

FIGURE 3.11

Weak ties connecting two cliques

(a) strong ties are unlikely to serve as bridges between cliques, and (b) not all weak ties will be bridges. Weak ties are more likely to be bridges because of the absence of pressures towards balance.

The original work that sparked the strength-of-weak-tie hypothesis showed that, for a random sample of recent professional, technical and managerial job changers living in a Boston suburb, of those 54 people finding a job through a person in their social networks, 16.7 per cent reported frequent contact with the person, 55.6 per cent occasional contact, and 27.8 per cent rare contact. Weak ties (involving occasional or rare contact) tended to be with people such as old college friends or former work colleagues with whom sporadic contact had been maintained (Granovetter, 1974).

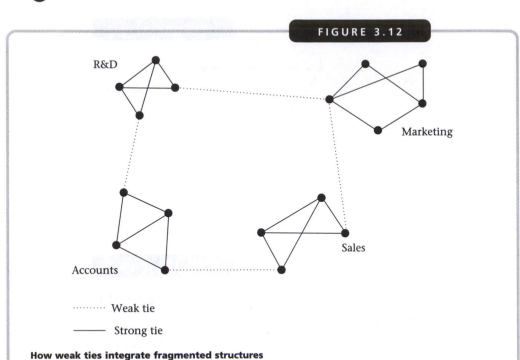

FIGURE 3.12

How weak ties integrate fragmented structures

The significance of weak ties goes beyond the transmission of important information between densely-structured cliques. Weak ties that bridge between cliques may knit fragmented structures together and permit organized action by members of a collectivity. Thus, if we consider the situation in Figure 3.12, there are four organizational groups with strong ties within the groups and weak ties between some of the groups. Without these weak ties, each person in the organization would experience the organization as cohesive (because each person is embedded in a set of strong-tie relationships), but the overall structure of the organization would be fragmented. Research suggests that organizations characterized by multiple unconnected cliques tend to experience high inter-clique conflict (Nelson, 1989). Thus, the concept of weak ties enables us to understand how dyadic links between individuals can contribute to the overall fragmentation or cohesiveness of whole organizations or communities of organizations.

Structural holes

Granovetter's argument, to the extent that it relies on balance theory, is sentiment-based. If strength of tie is defined in a way unrelated to emotional attachment, then the triad in Figure 3.9 is no longer forbidden for strong or weak ties. Recent research (Hansen, 1999) looking at ties between project teams defined

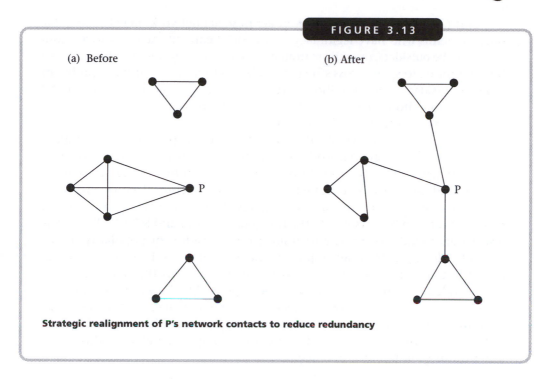

FIGURE 3.13

(a) Before (b) After

Strategic realignment of P's network contacts to reduce redundancy

tie strength in terms of more or less closeness and frequency of work contact at the group level. Teams with weak inter-unit ties were best able to transfer less complex knowledge, whereas teams with strong inter-unit ties were best able to transfer more complex knowledge. This work moves the strength-of-tie argument away from balance theory into contingency theory. Pressures towards balance are irrelevant. The only question is: What is the optimal mix of strong and weak ties to maximize work outcomes?

More generally, the weak-tie hypothesis has been recast as a question of social capital. Individual actors (people, sub-units, organizations) have been portrayed as seeking to increase their social capital by forging network ties that span between self-contained cliques. Structural-hole research focuses attention solely on the importance of bridging ties. According to this perspective, actors can leverage their investments in social relations by rearranging their networks as depicted in Figure 3.13: actor P reduces the redundancy of contacts by using three links to connect to three different cliques rather than sending all three links to one clique.

Recent work has suggested that the bridging ties illustrated in Figure 3.13 are subject to fairly rapid decay, especially for those actors with little experience in maintaining structural-hole advantages. In one study, only 10 per cent of ties defined as bridging in year one were considered bridging in the following year (Burt, 2002). Actors may therefore have to search continually for new structural holes to bridge in order to continue to gain information and resource advantages.

Burt (2000) suggests the role of broker in social networks may be advisable only for actors who have legitimacy in the social context. Actors who are considered to be outsiders, or who are from non-traditional groups, may be punished for attempting to span across structural holes. Actors with legitimacy problems (due to outsider or non-traditional status) may have to borrow social capital from structural-hole-spanning sponsors rather than trying to broker information and resources themselves (Burt, 2000).

But other research suggests that borrowing social capital from a prestigious actor may be a strategy that works for all actors, not just for those with legitimacy problems. One study of 36 business units within a $6 billion family-owned food company investigated the transfer of technical knowledge with respect to one block of units run by members of the ruling family and another block of units run by outsiders to the ruling family (Tsai and Kilduff, 2002). The researchers found two important results: (1) a position of popularity in the opposite block predicted an improvement of business unit performance; (2) both the units in the family-run block and the units in the non-family-run block tended to achieve popularity in the opposite block by forging a tie with a prestigious unit in the opposite block. Thus, the same heterophilous strategy of connecting with a prestigious member of the opposite block worked equally well for those with high status in this context (family-run units) and those with lesser status (non-family-run units).

Structural Role Theory

Structural cohesion

The network approach to social evaluation has brought new life to the old questions: To whom do I compare myself? To whose opinions do I pay attention? Whose behaviours are likely to influence mine? The work on cliques suggested that people were influenced by those with whom they shared strong bonds of friendship or communication. As we have seen in our discussion of the Hawthorne studies and Simmelian ties, people in cliques tend to develop and enforce norms that tend to standardize attitudes and behaviour. From a network perspective, two members of a clique are structurally cohesive in the sense that they are both constrained by the structure of the group of which they are members. This notion of structural cohesion can be extended to include actors in sub-groups (such as the k-plexes and n-cliques discussed above on pp. 46–7): irrespective of their feelings for each other, two actors (such as C and D in Figure 3.14), who are reachable by a common set of other actors in the sub-group, are pressured by these other actors to think and behave in similar ways (Friedkin, 1998: 69–70).

Structural equivalence and role equivalence

From a network equivalence perspective, two actors may pay close attention to each other, not because they are embedded in a cohesive group, but because

FIGURE 3.14

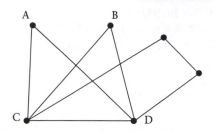

Actors A and B are structurally equivalent; C and D are structurally cohesive

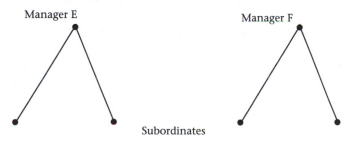

Managers E and F are role equivalent

Structural equivalence, structural cohesion and role equivalence compared

(a) they play similar roles in the same network, or (b) they play similar roles in different networks. Actors, such as A and B in Figure 3.14, who are substitutable for each other in the sense of having precisely the same relations with other actors in the same network, are said to be structurally equivalent. For example, two subordinates who work for the same supervisor and have the same set of peers are, from a structural perspective, occupying the same position in the network, and are therefore structurally equivalent (Lorrain and White, 1971). In a similar vein we can picture two individuals who work in different departments, have different supervisors and different peers. But the structure of their relationships may be highly similar, much as two fathers of teenage sons may appear to be highly similar in the structure of their relationships. Actors occupying similar positions but in different networks (such as managers E and F in Figure 3.14) are said to be role equivalent (see Krackhardt and Porter, 1986, for an example).

Although the distinction between role equivalence and either structural equivalence or structural cohesion is relatively easy to discern given that role equivalence refers to a comparison between networks rather than within a network, the task of discerning the difference between structural cohesion and structural equivalence has proven more difficult. For example, a re-analysis of partial data from a study of the adoption of an antibiotic drug by small medical practices in Illinois appeared to show conclusively that physicians adopted because their structurally-equivalent peers had adopted (Burt, 1987). A re-analysis of the same data using an analysis that took into account the actual date of adoption rejected this conclusion and claimed to show no social network effects (Marsden and Podolny, 1990). Yet another re-analysis, making slightly different assumptions, showed that both structural cohesion and structural equivalence affected adoption (Strang and Tuma, 1993), but this finding was overturned by another study of the data showing no social network effects if marketing pressure by drug companies was considered (Van der Bulte and Lilien, 2001).

At the very least, therefore, we can conclude that it is easy to confuse structural cohesion and structural equivalence effects. The decision to emphasize one rather than another can be guided by what makes most sense given a specific social context. If the context is one in which the researcher expects to find solidarity among colleagues, people helping each other, norms of cooperation and so on, then a structural cohesion approach is warranted. If, in contrast, the context is one where the researcher expects to find an emphasis on competition between members of different statuses or groups, then a structural equivalence or role equivalence approach can be useful.

Under some circumstances one approach may be preferred over the other based on the characteristics of the data. For example, in an organization that includes supervisors and subordinates, structurally-equivalent actors are likely to be found either among the set of supervisors or among the set of subordinates. Supervisors and subordinates are unlikely to be structurally equivalent with each other given the different lateral and horizontal relations in which actors playing these different roles engage. But a supervisor and a subordinate may well be structurally cohesive (without being structurally equivalent) in the sense of forming a dyad within which social influence flows from one person to another based on relationships of power and liking (Marsden and Friedkin, 1993).

Let us look at an example of how the cohesion and structural equivalence approaches help illuminate social dynamics. An analysis of friendship relations among the French financial elite used standard algorithms to examine cliques, n-cliques and K-plexes (Kadushin, 1995). Several overlapping small clusters of people were detected. Together these overlapping clusters incorporated nearly the whole network, revealing a core–periphery structure.

Using structural equivalence algorithms to examine friendship links between clusters of people, Kadushin found that the elite network could be divided into two blocks. To detect blocks, he used several algorithms, including CONCOR (Breiger et al., 1975), which detects blocks of actors who have similar relations to other actors by successively correlating the rows within (in this case) a symmetrized friendship matrix until all values reach either +1 or −1. The algorithm divides the social world into two groups. As Barley (1990: 96) summarized the results of this technique: 'Members of each group have a pattern of ties that is maximally similar to each other and maximally different from members of the other group.' Once two blocks are identified, the algorithm returns to the original matrix and, using the blocks that have been identified, splits these blocks into smaller blocks, and so on. The researcher then selects the block partitioning result that best represents the data. (See Scott, 2000: 131–9, for more details concerning this technique.)

The results of Kadushin's blockmodelling showed that, in the case of the French financial elite, within each of two blocks, friendship densities were high, but between each block densities were relatively low. His results are consistent with both a cohesion and a structural equivalence interpretation. Cohesion within each block was important, as was rivalry between the two blocks. It is important to note that the identification of very low densities (or 'structural holes') between blocks is one of the most critical network steps. (We discussed the importance of structural holes in greater depth on pages 28–30 and 56–8 above.)

EXPORTING NETWORK IDEAS INTO ORGANIZATION THEORY: TOWARDS A CRITICAL SYNTHESIS

Several organization theories have long incorporated network ideas and methods in their conceptualizations and tests. For example, the concept of the negotiated environment (Cyert and March, 1963; Emery and Trist, 1965) between organizations has played a starring role in both contingency theory (Thompson, 1967) and resource dependence theory (Pfeffer and Salancik, 1978) and lends itself to operationalization in terms of relationships between organizations (as interlocking directorates, for example – see Burt, 1983). The extent to which a focal organization negotiates its environment in terms of resource flows with other organizations can be examined through an analysis of the network of relationships in which the organization is embedded. The idea has been extended by institutional theorists to the whole organizational field through the concept of isomorphism between organizational actors engaged in processes of coercion, mimesis and normative influence (DiMaggio and Powell, 1983). Research suggests that organizations retain considerable latitude to negotiate the extent to which their goals and structures become isomorphic with their network partners (Oliver, 1988). Thus, the network perspective brings strategic choice back into the sometimes overly deterministic emphases of the ecological and institutional views. We trace the emergence of a synthesis between network approaches and such contemporary organization perspectives as resource dependence, contingency theory, population ecology, transaction cost economics, and the knowledge-based view of the firm.

Social network research has given new dynamism to contingency theory. Much exciting work from a network perspective explicitly involves a contingency logic such as the discovery that strong ties are good for the transfer of complex knowledge whereas weak ties are good for more codified knowledge (Hansen, 1999) and the analysis of how technology can differentially affect structure depending on the nature of social ties in the workplace (Barley, 1990). An implicit contingency logic also underlies the analysis of how spanning across structural holes differentially aids certain types of people (e.g., men more than women – Burt, 1992) and certain personality types (e.g., Mehra et al., 2001). As discussions of the network organization as a distinct organizational form continue, we await a full-blown contingency theory analysis of how trust-based coordinating mechanisms facilitate differentiation and integration.

It is with the resource dependence approach that social networkers have engaged in the most intellectual traffic and borrowing. Whereas the resource dependence approach emphasizes the importance of stable flows of resources, the social network approach has opened up questions concerning how the focal organization should optimize its portfolio of ties with resource partners. From a resource dependence perspective, the general importance of the focal organization establishing a pattern of interconnectedness has long been recognized (e.g., Pfeffer and Salancik, 1978: 68). We find continued development of this idea in recent social network research that discusses the liability of unconnectedness for firms in the biotechnology industry (Powell et al., 1996). But going beyond whether the focal firm has connections or not is the question of whether the firm's connections are with closely-aligned partners or whether they consist of arm's length market relationships. Recent social network research has suggested that firms will tend to survive longer if they have a strong relationship to a network of both close and arm's length partners (Uzzi, 1996). Further, firms can dramatically change their dependencies in the environment by forging synergistic alliances that can produce rapid gains in profitability (Larson, 1992).

Resource dependence notions of interconnectedness and constraint continue to spur research that looks not at the focal organization but at the whole organizational field. More recent work that collects together many of these concepts derives from complexity theory, an approach that eschews the single organizational focus in preference for analyses at the level of the organizational field. From a complexity perspective, under-connected fields tend to be too disorganized to adapt to environmental changes, partially connected (or loosely coupled) actors constitute adaptive fields, whereas over-connected (or tightly coupled) actors constitute gridlocked fields (Eisehnardt and Bhatia, 2002).

Population ecology intersects with social network research in several interesting areas. Central concepts in population ecology such as legitimacy, competition and niche can be examined using network ideas and methods. The legitimacy of a firm is related to the firm's network connections in the market (Hannan and Freeman, 1977; Poldony, 1993; Podolny et al., 1996). The emphasis on competition in population ecology is similar to the idea of structural equivalence in a network (Burt, 1987). As Oliver (1988: 549) noted, the population ecology idea of organizations sharing a common 'form' relates precisely to the notion of structurally equivalent organizations. The network image of a market is analogous to the population ecology image of a niche (Burt, 1992). In addition, the structural inertia assumption in population ecology is closely related to the idea of constraint in network research. There is potential for contrasts and syntheses between network and ecological approaches to organizations. The emerging ecological view is that organizational evolution can best be studied by examining social processes, environmental conditions, and interactions within and among populations (Baum and Singh, 1994). Given the convergence of interests between social network and ecological research, we expect to see more work devoted to theory development in this emerging area.

Transaction cost economics is perhaps the favourite whipping boy for social network researchers. It has been accused of offering an under-socialized perspective of actors (Granovetter, 1985), of being bad for managers (Ghoshal and Moran, 1996), and of neglecting the importance of distinctive organizational forms such as a market and hierarchy hybrid (Baker, 1990; Powell, 1990). Lost in this criticism is the fact that the transaction costs approach theoretically focuses attention on ties between actors – transactions – and thus is inherently compatible with network logic. A similar point could be made concerning agency theory that views the firm as a nexus of contracts, a region dense with formal and informal ties between suppliers, customers and partners. A network approach to transactions and contracts could potentially illuminate patterns of ties focused not on *actors* but on *interactions* constituted as transactions or as contracts.

Social network research has also contributed to the burgeoning literature that views the firm as a body of knowledge. The knowledge-based view of the firm emphasizes that the accumulation and application of knowledge builds organizational capabilities (e.g., Grant, 1996). A social network approach helps explain how organizational knowledge is accumulated and applied. Networks are not just relationships that govern the diffusion of innovative ideas or explain the variability of access to information across competing firms. Networks within and between organizations also constitute the capabilities that can generate economic rents and augment the value of firms (Kogut, 2000). Network research has cast doubt on the idea promulgated by March and Simon (1958) that the division of labour and simplification of work within bureaucratic organization is a solution to the individual's bounded rationality. Complex knowledge emerges not from work simplification but from the social interactions of individuals within and across organizations (Brown and Duguid, 2000). Innovations are likely to be located in the 'interstices between firms, universities, research laboratories, suppliers and customers' (Powell et al., 1996). More research is needed not on the simplification of work into easily-controlled bureaucratic routines, but on the importance for knowledge creation of coordinated routines of 'synergistic partnering' between informally-connected organizations (Powell et al., 1996). Examining the networks that constitute the firm and the interorganizational networks in which each firm is embedded can enrich the theory development of the knowledge-based view.

The emerging critical synthesis of network approaches and organizational theories contributes to strategy research in other areas besides the research-based perspective. For example, scholars have integrated social network approaches and resource dependence theory to study the formation of strategic alliances (e.g., Gulati, 1995) and various forms of interorganizational relationships (e.g., Baker, 1990). Research has also used network concepts to examine the emergence of new organizational forms (Podolny, 1998) and the new knowledge economy (Kogut, 2000). We expect to see more such creative syntheses applied to the strategy area.

SUMMARY

The evidence we reviewed shows that network theories relevant to organizations are flourishing. Our review suggests that network research on organizations tends to pursue one or more of three strategies: (a) the importation of theory from other disciplines such as mathematics and social psychology; (b) the use of home-grown theoretically-resonant concepts (such as strength of weak ties) from within the social network tradition; and (c) the export of network concepts into existing organizational theories to create hybrid approaches. The eclecticism of social network approaches militates against a unified programmatic theory of organizational networks. The challenge for research is to retain the distinctiveness of social network emphases on patterns of relations, multiple levels of analysis, and the integration of graphical and quantitative data. In the next chapter we delve into more detail concerning two fledgling theoretical approaches that are in the process of emerging from social psychology to help answer questions concerning individuals in organizational social networks.

RECOMMENDED FURTHER READING

Burt, R.S. 1992. *Structural holes: The social structure of competition.* Cambridge, MA: Harvard University Press.

A compelling and engaging synthesis of network ideas formulated around the idea of the strategic management of social ties. This book takes the notion of a structural hole (defined as 'the separation between nonredundant contacts') and applies it at different levels of analysis to argue that actors who span strategically across disconnected links tend to gain information and control advantages that show up as fast-track promotions (individuals) or higher profits (firms).

Granovetter, M. 1973. The strength of weak ties. *American Journal of Sociology*, 78: 1360–80.

Granovetter, M.S. 1985. Economic action and social structure: The problem of embeddedness. *American Journal of Sociology*, 91: 481–510.

These two articles by Granovetter establish much of the theory that has fuelled the surge in network research on organizations, and are required reading for anyone interested in social network theory.

Monge, P.R. and Contractor, N.S. 1999. Emergence of communication networks. In F.M. Jablin and L.I. Putnam (eds), *The new handbook of organizational communication: Advances in theory, research, and methods*, pp. 440–502. Thousand Oaks, CA: Sage.

A comprehensive survey of theories that have been used in social network research, together with a review of relevant work.

4 In Pursuit of Lost Questions: Bridging the Gap between Structuralist and Individualist Approaches to Social Networks

The social network approach offers, as one of its several attractions, the possibility of helping us understand how individual actors create, maintain, exploit, and are constrained by social structures at several levels of analysis, including the group, the department, the organization and the interorganizational environment. The potential is there for researchers to examine not just the often discussed micro–macro linkages between individual action and social structure, but the ways in which networks of relationships at one level are embedded within and articulate networks at other levels. The network approach is sometimes referred to as 'structural analysis' because of this overwhelmingly structural focus on the interdependence of social units within fields of influence that cross levels and traditional boundaries.

That the social network approach has not fulfilled its promise to explicate the dynamic interplay of social structures across levels and boundaries is due to several factors. Over 20 years ago one commentator decried the tendency in network analysis towards 'overelaboration of technique and data and an accumulation of trivial results' (Boissevain, 1979: 393). More recently, commentators have praised the 'high degree of technical sophistication' of the network approach (Emirbayer and Goodwin, 1994: 1411) while bemoaning the absence of 'a fully adequate explanatory model for the actual formation, reproduction, and transformation of social networks themselves' (Emirbayer and Goodwin,

1994: 1413). There is a consistent criticism that the network approach is focused on techniques and statistical models and neglectful of the ways in which micro-level structure connects to 'any larger substantive part of social life' (Granovetter, 1979: 507–8).

An obsessive interest in technical issues is not the only factor that has diverted social network researchers from addressing micro–macro connections and network dynamics. A further reason for the neglect is the basic orientation of network research towards static social structures and away from active individual actors. Scholars who study the structure of networks tend to ignore the attributes of actors (such as personality) because outcomes are assumed to derive from embeddedness in systems of relations. The focus on the analysis and description of structures of relations has tended to produce a view of networks as static entities that have an inherent interest as features of the social world. In organizational studies, there have been impatient calls for the social network approach to go beyond telling us how, for example, structural holes can be 'used to advantage' and begin to address 'the appearance and disappearance of structural holes' themselves (Salancik, 1995: 349). To understand how structure changes over time, the analysis of individual actor attributes, motivations, cognitions and behaviours in actual social contexts such as organizations may be helpful.

In this chapter and the next chapter we address issues of micro–macro links and network dynamics respectively. We start in this chapter by bringing individual actors back into structural analysis through a discussion of how actors' cognitions and personality influence and are influenced by networks. Our focus is unabashedly on the complexities of real people in real-world contexts.

STRUCTURAL ANALYSIS AND INDIVIDUAL ACTOR DIFFERENCES

The apparently innocuous idea that individuals help shape the social networks within which they are embedded is regarded by some as contrary to the structural legacy within which many social network researchers work. Inspired by Durkheimian sociology, some researchers have proclaimed their adherence to a version of structuralism that denies any agency to individuals in the creation and maintenance of collective structures. The analogy often suggested is with language: language (like a social network) connects people together, permits communication and transactions, and is a social fact that has a reality independent of any of the actors connected by the language. Radical structuralists point out that individuals engage in constant action (speaking the language) even though none of these individuals can be said to have contributed to the structure in which their actions are embedded (i.e., none of them created the language they speak). Language (like other social structures) exists, it is argued, as a supra-individual institution, relatively independent of any single individual's motivations or attributes.

Building from this position, structuralists have tended to ignore the possibility that actors' attributes, cognitions or personalities shape social networks. Indeed, some social network researchers, in their eagerness to build a distinctive field of study, have made a career not just of neglecting individual agency, but of claiming to go beyond the study of individuals altogether. Let us look at some representative quotes from major network theorists. The study of individuals is a 'dead end' (Mayhew, 1980: 335); the unit of analysis in network studies is 'the social network, never the individual' (Mayhew, 1980: 349); structuralists have tended to 'shun the "person" construct as polluting' (White, 1992: 3); sociologists have been 'misled … into studying the *attributes* of aggregated sets of *individuals* rather than the structural nature of social systems' (Wellman, 1988a: 15). These quotes signal the belief among many network researchers that their approach to social science represents a 'scientific revolution' (Berkowitz, 1982: 150) that may be incommensurable with other more individualistic approaches to social science (Mayhew, 1980: 339).

The analogy between inherited institutions such as the Dutch language and collective social phenomena such as social networks is a tenuous one. Whereas the Dutch language existed before its current speakers were born and will outlive them, a specific social network may radically change its structure if only one actor departs.

Consider Figure 4.1. The removal of actor A would result in the network fragmenting into two disconnected parts. Clearly, the presence of this particular actor in this particular network makes a difference to how the network functions. Theory and research concerning how individuals and the positions they hold reciprocally influence each other can help answer questions concerning the origins of social structure and the effects of social structure on individual cognitions and attributes.

The study of such individual attributes, however, calls forth various degrees of scorn and dismissal from network researchers. Network researchers tend to be united in their adherence to what critics have called the *anti-categorical imperative*. This imperative, 'rejects all attempts to explain human behavior or social processes solely in terms of the categorical attributes of actors, whether individual or collective' (Emirbayer and Goodwin, 1994: 1414). The typical start to any social network article often involves a ritualistic swipe at those who have previously focused on the attributes of individuals. Thus, the first line in a celebrated network approach to attitude formation begins, 'Most social studies explain individual attitudes in terms of individual attributes' and continues with a reference to the 'small proportion' of the variance explained by attribute-based approaches (Erickson, 1988: 99). Invisible attributes of individuals (such as cognitions, tastes, attitudes, dispositions, and so

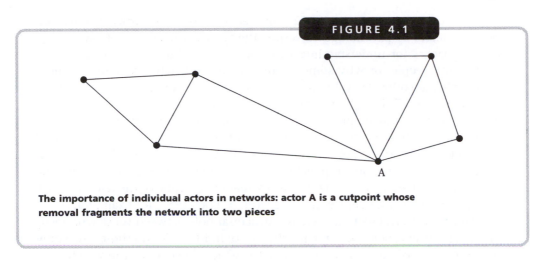

FIGURE 4.1

A

The importance of individual actors in networks: actor A is a cutpoint whose removal fragments the network into two pieces

on) have been dismissed as difficult to measure (e.g., Pfeffer, 1983) or unnecessary to measure given a network approach (e.g., McPherson, et al., 1992: 168). The most incendiary attack on such attribute-based research simply declared that, 'Individualists have substituted platitudes as non-answers to their non-questions' (Mayhew, 1980: 365).

The questions we raise are therefore likely to be regarded by some network researchers as 'non-questions' given the somewhat heretical emphasis on individual cognition, agency and personality. Many network researchers appear to have adopted a naive version of behaviourism that focuses on '*concrete* social relations among specific social actors' (Wellman and Berkowitz, 1988: 5) to the exclusion not just of 'symbols, meanings, and values' (Wellman and Berkowitz, 1988: 5), but also of cognition (Boorman and White, 1976: 1442). This emphasis on the concrete and the exclusion of unobservable cognitions, traits and dispositions is not accidental but is quite programmatic as the statement by Granovetter concerning the 'Structural analysis in the social sciences' book series makes clear: 'The series ... will present approaches that explain social behavior and institutions by reference to relations among such concrete social entities as persons and organizations. This contrasts with ... explanations stressing the causal primacy of abstract concepts such as ideas, values, mental harmonies and cognitive maps.' (The statement occurs opposite the title page in each book in the series – e.g., Hage and Harary, 1996: ii.) Researchers in this tradition pride themselves on being able to state that 'no assumption of individual differences is necessary to explain the emergence of social differentiation' (Mark, 1998: 309), preferring to violate the obvious (individuals have different endowments) in their adherence to the dubious (ethnic differences are the result of differences in technological systems).

Questions concerning individual differences in network structure have also been neglected by psychologists. Despite the apparent relevance of psychological approaches for understanding why some people build different networks from other people, or why some people can exploit network resources more effectively than others, psychologists tend to ignore the existence of social structures altogether. One of the most disheartening aspects of the psychology literature is to find articles purportedly about social networks that evidence no connection at all with the social network studies appearing in sociological and organizational journals. For example, a recent study (Agnew et al., 2001) concerning how the relationship between two individuals was affected by the couple's embeddedness in social networks, referenced none of the relevant work in the social network field (such as the work of Bott, 1957, for example).

Our review suggests that there is a structural hole between those who focus on social networks but ignore the psychology of individuals and those who study the psychology of individuals but ignore the social networks within which individuals are embedded. As organizational social network researchers, we are bound by no disciplinary dogma and can therefore freely borrow from the structural and psychological traditions in pursuit of answers to important questions. In this section, we examine two boundary-spanning perspectives that can help us explore the complex effects of individuals on social structure and social structure on individuals: cognitive network theory (addressing issues of individual cognition and social networks); and an emergent theory of personality and social structure (addressing issues of individual dispositions and social networks).

COGNITIVE NETWORK THEORY

Cognitions are unobservable and distinctly individual in that they reside inside the heads of individuals. Further, the study of cognition is the province of psychology whereas network research has tended to be associated with sociology and anthropology. For these reasons, theory and research concerning cognition and social networks might appear paradoxical or unpromising. However, an emerging perspective, that we call cognitive network theory, has examined individual actors' perceptions of social networks, how such perceptions influence the formation of social networks, and the reciprocal influence of networks on cognition. Key concepts include cognitive balance, cognitive accuracy, and cognitive maps.

Cognitive Balance

At the height of his wealth and success, the financier Baron de Rothschild was petitioned for a loan by an acquaintance. Reputedly, the great man replied, 'I won't give you a loan myself; but I will walk arm-in-arm with you across the floor of the Stock Exchange, and you will soon have willing lenders to spare'. (Cialdini, 1989: 45)

We all know the old expression that, 'You are known by the company you keep'. If you are perceived to be a friend of the Baron de Rothschild, then members of the London Stock Exchange are likely to upgrade their evaluation of your creditworthiness in a process some have dubbed 'basking in reflected glory' (Cialdini, 1989). Research has shown that the benefit of having a prominent friend in an organization derives from others' perceptions of who your friends are. As Baron Rothschild realized, for some purposes, it doesn't matter whether you really have prominent friends. What matters is whether people think you have prominent friends. Specifically, building from Heider's (1958) study on cognitive balance, researchers found that being perceived to have a prominent friend in an organization boosted an individual's reputation as a good performer, whereas actually having such a friend had no effect (Kilduff and Krackhardt, 1994).

An emphasis on the importance of individual cognitions of this kind has been a feature of the social network perspective from the beginning. Kurt Lewin, for example, emphasized that changes in the social relationships surrounding the individual could only be predicted by considering the subjective probabilities in the mind of each individual: 'This basic principle makes the subjective probability of an event a part of the life space of that individual. But it excludes the objective probability of alien factors that cannot be derived from the life space' (Lewin, 1951: 59). Similarly, Fritz Heider (1958) developed a theory of interpersonal balance premised on the importance of considering the ways in which individuals perceived the relationships in which they were involved. This emphasis on perceived relationships underlies the structural theory of action developed by Burt (1982: 176): 'An actor's evaluations are affected by others to the extent that he perceives them to be socially similar to himself.' But this assumption – that structurally equivalent actors perceive each other as similar – is seldom tested. More recent research indicates that structural equivalence may not be a good proxy for perceived similarity (Kilduff, 1990; Michaelson and Contractor, 1992).

Fritz Heider did the most to provide a systematic account of the ways in which individuals made sense of their relationships. For our purposes, his work can be summarized in the idea of the balance schema – the tendency for people to perceive sentiment relations (such as friendship) as both symmetric and transitive. Symmetry refers to the perceiver's assumption that friendship relations will be reciprocated. Thus, if the perceiver sees that A chooses B as a friend, the perceiver will anticipate that B will also choose A as a friend. Transitivity refers to the perceiver's assumption that friendship relations will be complete. Thus, if the perceiver knows both that A is friends with B and that A is friends with C, the perceiver will anticipate that B and C will also be friends.

The balance schema consists of a set of cognitive expectations concerning the likely structure of the social world in terms of reciprocity and transitivity. The literature relating to cognitive balance is quite large (see Crockett, 1982; and Wasserman and Faust, 1994, for reviews). We focus here on that small part of this literature that has relevance for organizational behaviour. In particular, we present a detailed summary of recent research that offers a unifying model of perceived balance in organizational friendship networks (Krackhardt and Kilduff, 1999).

Individuals who perceive that their own friendship relations in organizations are unbalanced may react with strong emotions rather than with cool analytical reasoning. The balance schema, from this perspective, functions as a deep-seated goal of human interaction (see the discussions in D'Andrade, 1992; and Fiske, 1992). People strive to see their own friendship relations as balanced because the perception of unbalance induces feelings of uncertainty, instability (Festinger and Hutte, 1954) and nervousness (Sampson and Insko, 1964).

For friendship relations close to the individual, ego has the power to influence directly whether these relationships are balanced or not. If, for example, Jane finds that her attempts at friendship with Ruby are unrequited, then Jane can sever the friendship link or try even harder to elicit tokens of friendship from Ruby. Ego has considerable potential power to balance friendship relations through direct action of this sort. Similarly, if Jane finds that her friendships with Alice and Shirley have failed to bring Alice and Shirley together as friends, then Jane can act as matchmaker – arranging a joint lunch in the cafeteria, for example.

For relations close to ego, therefore, motivation is strong to balance relationships, and ego has the power to impose balance. Previous research has shown that people will alter relations or cognitions to preserve balance in close relationships (Kumbasar et al., 1994; Newcomb, 1961), and that individuals seek out information that reduces dissonance while avoiding information that increases it (Erlich et al., 1957).

Considerable evidence indicates that people prefer balanced relations in general, even when they themselves are not directly connected to the individuals concerned (De Soto, 1960; Freeman, 1992). In the everyday world of work, individuals are frequently brought into contact with acquaintances whose friendship relations may be unbalanced. Individuals may be required to negotiate social pathways in organizations that are perceived to be unstructured and therefore problematic. Avoiding people with friendship problems may be either not possible or not compatible with a productive career.

Thus, to avoid emotional tension, individuals are likely to perceive their own close relationships as balanced. Ego has both the motivation and the power to arrange for these relationships to be balanced. As ego looks beyond the immediate circle of close friends, the emotional pressure to perceive relations as balanced is likely to diminish sharply. People are likely to be relatively unaffected by the perception of balance among those with whom they have no

FIGURE 4.2

(a) Ego sees alter as close, and alter's relations as balanced

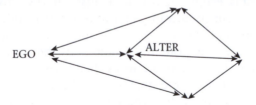

(b) Ego sees alter as at an intermediate distance, and
alter's relations as unbalanced

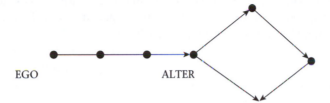

(c) Ego sees alter as far away, and alter's
relations as balanced

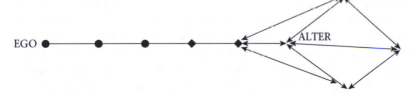

Curvilinear relationship between social distance and perceived balance

friendship ties. If ego is not directly involved, little discomfort results from perceived imbalance.

In a test of this prediction across four organizations, the results showed a decreasing probability for ego to perceive the friendship relations of alter as reciprocal and transitive as the perceived social distance between ego and alter increased from being relatively close to being in the middle distance. The perceived social distance was the shortest path, or geodesic, perceived by ego between ego and alter. Thus, the perceived social distance from ego to alter in Figure 4.2(b) is three.

According to the latest research on cognitive balance in organizations, however, this decreasing tendency to impose balance on perceived friendship links reverses as ego's gaze moves increasingly further outwards towards the periphery of the social world. People are cognitive misers in the sense that they rely on heuristics and short-cuts in forming opinions and perceptions (Dawes, 1976; Taylor, 1981; Taylor and Fiske, 1978). People may avoid expending cognitive energy keeping track of the potential relations in the organizations in which they work. To the extent that an individual uses a well-developed schema, many details of the social world may be filled in by the schema rather than derived from actual perception (see the review by Mandler, 1979). The balance schema provides ego with a way to infer the existence of relations when information is incomplete (Freeman, 1992). As people consider the friendship relations of those increasingly distant from themselves, they will have less and less knowledge of possible unbalanced relations. The farther away the relationship, the less information ego has regarding it and the more likely ego is to assume the relations are balanced (Kuethe, 1962).

Thus, the balance schema may be imposed on close relations (to avoid emotional tension) and attributed to the friendship relations of distant others (to fill in the blanks in social knowledge). The composite model of perceived balance suggests that there will be a curvilinear relationship between social distance from ego and the degree of balance perceived. Results across four organizations supported this model for perceptions of reciprocity and transitivity (Krackhardt and Kilduff, 1999).

The relationships between perceived social distance and perceived balance are illustrated in Figure 4.2. In parts (a) and (c) of the figure, ego tends to perceive alter's friendship relations as balanced (reciprocated and transitive). In part (a) alter is perceived by ego as a personal friend, the social distance between them is close, and therefore there is a tendency for ego to reduce emotional tension by perceiving the relations of alter as balanced. In part (c) alter is perceived by ego as a friend of a friend of a friend of a friend, the social distance between ego and alter is far, and therefore there is a tendency for ego to rely on the balance schema to fill in the blanks in ego's knowledge about alter's relations: alter's relations are seen as balanced because of the cognitive miser effect. In part (b) alter is perceived by ego as a friend of a friend, the social distance between ego and alter is intermediate. Neither emotional tension nor the balance schema are invoked, and therefore ego tends to see more intransitivity in alter's relations under this scenario than in either (a) or (c).

Future work could focus on the intermediate distance just beyond ego's own perceived friendship circle where ego is likely to be troubled by persistent imbalance. In this middle area, ego has no power to act decisively to change relationships, and ego may know too much about the relations of these people on the margins of ego's world to be able to bias their relations cognitively using the principles of balance. Ego is likely to be unhappy at work to the extent that he or she perceives relations in the middle distance as unbalanced.

Unbalanced relationships represent not merely stress-producing features of the social world, but also structural holes to be bridged (see the discussion in Burt, 1992). People who perceive many unbalanced relationships in the middle distance may be both under cognitive strain and faced with alluring opportunities to bridge gaps. Further, people who report considerable experience with unbalanced social networks in organizations appear to be better able to spot structural holes in unfamiliar social settings and thereby forge more useful coalitions (Janicik, 2000). The perception of unbalance may therefore promote strategic tie formation.

The Organization as a Network of Cognitions

Cognitive balance theory as applied to organizations is compatible with a perspective that focuses on the organization as a network of cognitions. From this perspective, important concepts such as organization and environment 'are stored in the minds of participants … what ties an organization together is what ties thought together' (Bougon et al., 1977: 626). Cognitive organization theory asks questions such as: What is the effect of the social network on the cognitions of members? How do cognitions about the network affect organizational outcomes?

In one of the first examinations of how social networks affect cognition in an organization, Sampson (1968) found different patterns of cognitive change depending on the social relationships between organizational members. The research investigated people's perceptions of an ambiguous environmental stimulus – a spot of light in a dark room that gave the illusion of moving (the famous autokinetic effect first investigated by Sherif, 1936). Sampson paired up organizational members whose cognitions concerning how far the light appeared to move were moderately different. Social equals, with little previous interaction, tended to change their perceptions towards consensus concerning the distance the light appeared to move. Consensus was reached by the two people agreeing on an estimate that was mid-way between their two original estimates. By contrast, social unequals (one person expressing esteem for the other that was not reciprocated) who were well acquainted demonstrated cognitive deference. The esteemed person's perceptions tended initially to change towards a compromise position only to return to original estimates. Sampson described this process as follows: the esteemed person dragged 'the esteemer along with him in a pattern of true leadership which, according to the interview data, was not a conscious ploy on the esteemed's part' (Sampson, 1968: 415). Finally, Sampson looked at pairs composed of people who expressed mutual disesteem, with one member possessing hierarchical power over the other: 'After an approach tendency, a boomerang effect occurred … those in power hardly altered their judgments whereas the subordinates yielded markedly at first, but thereupon recoiled' (Sampson, 1968: 418). A later examination of the influence of the organizational network on cognition echoed Sampson's finding: 'In a dependence relationship, the less powerful member is likely to be forced to adapt the cognitive perspective of the more powerful member' (Walker, 1985: 107). Sampson's pioneering work on the ways in which social relationships and hierarchical differences affect perceptions of the changes in the environment has been overlooked by organizational researchers. According to his results, social networks literally help determine the visual images that organizational members perceive.

In another examination of the effect of perceived social relationships on organizational outcomes, a positive set of cognitions resulted from negative events. The researchers found that the closer that individuals perceived themselves to be to co-workers who had left the organization, the more satisfied and committed the individuals became (Krackhardt and Porter, 1985). Perhaps the turnover of a co-worker removed a source of negative information about the organization, or perhaps, as the authors suggest, the employees who stayed had to justify remaining by inflating their work-related attitudes.

The importance of perceived friendships was underscored in another study that examined job satisfaction. The researchers found that the more people disagreed with their friends in their perceptions of fellow employees on a series of seven key organizational dimensions, the more people were dissatisfied with their work (Krackhardt and Kilduff, 1990). In this study, the organization was explicitly examined as a cognitive system negotiated between interacting individuals who created locally-shared systems of meaning. The organization was depicted as a magnetic field in which individual components attracted and repelled each other, with friends mutually reinforcing interpretative systems. The question that remains unanswered in all of these studies, however, is: What if the individual's interpretative system is inaccurate?

Cognitive Accuracy

Cognitive network theory focuses on perceptions of networks, but there is a long-standing interest in comparing perceptions with measures of reality. For example, the Hawthorne researchers commented that employee work behaviour was controlled to a 'considerable extent' by sentiments and feelings concerning issues such as position in the work group, and that management 'frequently had to act in ignorance of these sentiments' resulting in 'many unforeseen consequences' (Roethlisberger and Dickson, 1939: 582).

A dramatic case study of unforeseen consequences of inaccurate management perceptions of the social network was described by Burt and Ronchi (1990), who were asked to assist the beleaguered CEO of a medium-sized American manufacturing firm. The authors paint the picture of the CEO's situation as follows:

> ... your employees hate you. ... Shared disdain for you brings other people together. Projects originating in your office consistently fail for want of proper implementation. Sensitive opinions expressed in meetings with your senior management are common shop knowledge within a week. The problem has followed you home in a way rarely experienced by American executives. You and your family have received bomb threats. (Burt and Ronchi,1990: 121).

The CEO was part of a management team that had taken over a non-profitable firm and restored it to record profits. But the new management did not know that, over the 33-year life of the company, relatives and friends of existing employees had been increasingly recruited to fill vacancies. The management knew only that new recruits tended to show up on Monday mornings 'like lemmings coming over the hill', to quote the CEO. Hidden from management view was the fact that existing employees were busy ensuring that their relatives and friends were first in line when vacancies were announced. One long-term employee, Bill Glass, had personally recruited 106 people in this way. Glass was fired during a routine cost-benefit analysis by a management that was unaware of his powerful position in the informal network. The rejected ex-worker actively promoted hostility against the firm's management.

In this case study, we see the dramatic consequences that can result from differing perceptions of the social structure of the organization. Research suggests that individuals can have dramatically different perceptions of the same network structure (Kilduff and Krackhardt, 1994). Further, those with more accurate cognitive maps of relevant social networks (such as the work advice network) tend to be perceived as more powerful by their fellow employees (Krackhardt, 1990). We now turn to an explicit consideration of cognitive maps.

Cognitive maps

What is a cognitive map? It is an individual representation of relations within a system of connections (Weick and Bougon, 1986: 105–6). An individual's cognitive map of a friendship network consists of the individual's picture of who is a friend with whom in a particular social system. Individuals are assumed to use these maps to negotiate their journeys through their social worlds.

These cognitive maps (also known as 'slices' – see Krackhardt, 1987) enable the researcher to determine many aspects of the individual's experience of the social world. For example, the individual's cognitive map can be analysed to see how much reciprocity and transitivity the individual perceives (e.g., Krackhardt and Kilduff, 1999). Also, the extent to which the individual perceives himself or herself as central in the network can be checked against the reports of others (e.g., Kumbasar et al., 1994). Similarly, the self-reported cognitive maps of two people assessed by conventional methods to be structurally equivalent can be checked to see if they actually perceive themselves to be equivalent (see Krackhardt, 1987: 116, for this and other suggestions).

The work of David Krackhardt on cognitive social structures (1987) has emphasized the importance of understanding individuals' cognitive maps. One of the major issues highlighted by Krackhardt is the discrepancy between how people perceive the social world and the actual pattern of relations existing in those worlds – as summarized earlier in this chapter (pp. 72–5), individuals are frequently biased in their perceptions (Kilduff and Krackhardt, 1994; Krackhardt and Kilduff, 1999; Kumbasar, et al., 1994).

How can we measure the actual pattern of friendship relations in an organization? To create the actual friendship map of network relations we must aggregate the information from individual cognitive maps. There are at least two ways to do this (Krackhardt, 1987). The first, referred to as Locally Aggregated Structure (LAS), asks two questions about every potential relationship between two actors in a social system: Does A think there is a link between A and B? Does B think there is a link between A and B? If we can assume that A and B are the people most likely to know whether a particular relationship (such as friendship) exists between them, then it makes sense to rely on these two actors for such information.

From the answers of A and B we can decide whether there is a 'real' friendship link between them, and whether this link is reciprocated. We can build up a map of the real network by aggregating information provided by all possible pairs of people in the social system. Note that this 'real' map preserves information on asymmetric ties. If both A and B agree that A considers B a friend but that B does not reciprocate this friendship, then this unreciprocated friendship link can be included in the 'real' map as a one-way arrow from A to B.

The second method by which social relations perceived by individuals can be aggregated into a composite map of the organization is by using the principle of consensus. A relation between A and B can be considered to exist if some percentage of the perceivers in the organization say that it exists. For example, one could specify the rule that: 'A relation exists from *i* to *j* if and only if a majority of the members of the network perceive that it exists' (Krackhardt, 1987: 118). This consensus method of determining the actual network map has been little used so far, but might be preferred to the LAS method under special circumstances. For example, we might use a consensus method for determining whether disreputable behavioural relations (such as gossiping or colluding) exist between two individuals. The consensus method might be more reliable than the reports of the individuals themselves, given the negative connotation of these kinds of relationship.

The promise of the cognitive approach to networks is that a better understanding of individuals' cognitions can help us understand the origins and formation of networks. In particular, we need research on how individuals' perceptions of social structures facilitate or hinder their enactment of such structures. Is it the case that those who are more accurate in their perceptions are also more able to take advantage of structural holes and other opportunities?

To what extent do perceptions of balance restrain people from changing their networks? That is, if an individual perceives himself or herself to be embedded in a balanced set of relationships, does this perception of balance constrain action that might destroy reciprocity and transitivity?

We also have little work that investigates whether those in positions of authority differentially influence the perceptions that others have of social networks. To the extent that there is bias in people's perceptions of network structure, is this bias purely egocentric (i.e., tending to exaggerate individuals' own centralities) or does it tend to magnify the importance of those in positions of power (see Johnson and Orbach, 2002)?

It seems to be generally believed that managers should have accurate perceptions of social networks so that they can delegate and coordinate effectively. But this belief has never been tested in organizational settings. What are the predictors and outcomes of accuracy in managerial perceptions of networks?

Finally, from a methodological perspective, is it possible to produce good representations of social networks by aggregating a sample of individual cognitive maps? In other areas of social science (such as anthropology) there is a tradition of relying on expert informants. Can the social network researcher discern the patterns of friendship and advice by asking a select group of experts in social structure? What distinguishes these experts in organizational settings?

AN EMERGENT THEORY OF PERSONALITY AND SOCIAL STRUCTURE

To speak of personality and social structure in the same breath is as close as one can get to heresy against the established social network paradigm. Whereas the study of network cognition has developed rapidly in recent years, the neglect of personality continues in network research. Thus, there are tremendous opportunities for linking individualist and structuralist paradigms of research, for bridging the micro/macro divide, and for understanding how individuals enact social structures in organizations. We outline here the beginnings of an emergent perspective on how stable personality traits shape the social network roles that individuals play in organizations, and we speculate concerning the possibility that some types of learned disposition may be affected by the occupancy of social network roles. We begin with a brief review of some of the earlier pioneering investigations that have been overlooked in the current structuralist thinking (e.g., Adorno et al., 1950; Breiger and Ennis, 1979; Newcomb, 1961) and then consider how self-monitoring orientation helps determine network roles in organizations. We conclude with a consideration of earlier sociological work on social personality, and offer some ideas for future network research from a personality perspective.

We should not assume that structuralists have nothing to say about the distinctiveness of individuals in social arenas. There are indeed some serious pioneering attempts to bridge the structural hole between individual and structuralist approaches. One attempt, co-authored by an early proponent of structural analysis, investigated whether individuals with certain types of interpersonal orientation tended to gravitate to certain positions identified on the basis of blockmodel analysis of social networks (Breiger and Ennis, 1979). This research recognized that blockmodel analysis as developed by structuralists (e.g., White et al., 1976) 'deliberately disavows the identification of personality types' (Breiger and Ennis, 1979: 262). But the authors persevered with their effort to understand how types of individual, identified on the basis of personality orientation, might coalesce in social structures identified on the basis of similarity of interaction patterns. The research found that personality types identified on the basis of reports from trained observers matched blocks of people identified on the basis of members' reports of ties. Thus, dominant-friendly individuals tended to occupy one block of structurally equivalent people, whereas dominant-hostile individuals tended to occupy another block. The social network analysis facilitated both the identification of personality types and the discovery of social ties between types. Similarly, the personality data helped 'expand and enrich blockmodel interpretations' (Breiger and Ennis, 1979: 269). The research suggested that individuals share with others both personality orientations and relational patterns. Identity, from this perspective, is a structured duality that incorporates both the dispositional and the relational.

Another pioneering investigator, in a celebrated study of membership in a college fraternity (Newcomb, 1961), examined the relationship between the personality trait authoritarianism (Adorno et al., 1949) and the ways in which people constructed personal networks. Authoritarians are distinguished by their negative views towards foreigners, their acceptance of the attitudes of those in power, and their beliefs concerning the subordination of women. This research found that authoritarianism tended to bias the accuracy of social perception. People with authoritarian personalities tended to overestimate the degree to which others, to whom they were attracted, shared their opinions and reciprocated their liking. Authoritarians therefore tended to build asymmetric social networks characterized by non-reciprocity in opinions and liking. Non-authoritarians tended to perceive more accurately who agreed with them and let their friendship choices follow these more accurate perceptions (Newcomb, 1961: 143). Newcomb's results paint a fascinating picture of flexible non-authoritarians preferring to affiliate with those who hold similar values to themselves, whereas authoritarians tend to bias their perceptions of others' beliefs systems in order to hold fast to the friendships they believe they have formed. This research is one of the first attempts, therefore, to trace the ways in which individuals' personality orientations contribute to social network formation in organizations.

More recent work emphasizing the social dispositional antecedents of networks in organizations has sought to understand how a stable personality trait (self-monitoring) predisposes individuals to structure their social worlds and occupy certain social roles in networks. This work specifically aims at bridging the gap between individualist and structuralist approaches in organizational settings. Self-monitoring research builds on Erving Goffman's (1959) insights concerning the advantages that accrue to those who adapt attitudes and behaviours to the demands of social contexts. These advantages include social approval, trust and liking. The concept of self-monitoring forms the basis for the systematic study of an individual's propensity to scan social environments for clues concerning appropriate expression and behaviour (Snyder, 1974, 1987). Individuals differ in the extent to which they are willing and able to monitor and control their self-expression in social situations. Some people resemble successful actors or politicians in their ability to find the appropriate words and behaviours for a range of quite different social situations. They present the right image for the right audience. Other people, by contrast, appear to take to heart the advice Polonius gave to Laertes in Shakespeare's *Hamlet*, 'To thine own self be true': They insist on being themselves, no matter how incongruent their self-expressions may be with the requirements of the social situation.

Research on self-monitoring has provided important insights into individual differences in how people present themselves in social contexts (see Snyder, 1987, for a review). Previous studies have distinguished between high self-monitors, who are attuned to role expectations, and low self-monitors, who insist on being themselves despite social expectations (Snyder, 1974). High self-monitors, identified by their high scores on the Self-Monitoring Scale (Snyder and Gangestad, 1986), are 'markedly sensitive and responsive to social and interpersonal cues to situational appropriateness', whereas low self-monitors are 'less responsive to situational and interpersonal specifications of appropriate behavior' (Snyder and Gangestad, 1982: 123). High self-monitors use cues from others for monitoring – that is, regulating and controlling – their verbal and non-verbal self-presentation (Snyder, 1979: 89). Low self-monitors, on the other hand, are 'controlled from within by their affective states and attitudes' (Snyder, 1979: 89). In a social situation, high self-monitors ask the following: 'Who does this situation want me to be and how can I be that person?' By contrast, low self-monitors ask: 'Who am I and how can I be me in this situation?' (Snyder, 1979).

Self-monitoring research therefore provides one answer to the age-old question of whether behaviour is a function of consistent dispositions or strong situational pressures. From a self-monitoring perspective, some individuals (the low self-monitors) are relatively consistent, demonstrating behaviour derived from inner feelings, attitudes and beliefs. Other individuals (the high self-monitors) are relatively flexible, adjusting behaviour to the demands of different situations. Self-monitoring orientation can be understood as a distinctive aspect of each individual's personality. Research on twins has suggested a possible genetic source of self-monitoring differences (Gangestad, 1984; Gangestad and Snyder, 1985). The proportions of high and low self-monitors in the population appear to be stable across generations of people (Gangestad and Snyder, 1985). Accumulating evidence 'suggests that self-monitoring is a stable personality trait throughout one's lifespan' (Jenkins, 1993: 84). Self-monitoring effects have been demonstrated on managerial promotions over a five-year period (Kilduff and Day, 1994).

Recent research (Mehra et al., 2001) suggests three distinct but mutually compatible models of how self-monitoring contributes to the structuring of social worlds; and how disposition and structure combine to influence important outcomes in organizations. The first model (the mediation model) suggests that high self-monitors, relative to lows, will tend to move into central positions in social networks in organizations and thereby benefit from the resources that flow to occupants of central positions. This model builds on research that shows high self-monitors playing different roles in different social groups and low self-monitors preferring to be with the same people across social activities. High self-monitors like to play tennis, chess and computer games with different people, whereas low self-monitors tend to engage in different activities with the same people (Snyder et al., 1983).

The second model (the interaction model) suggests that, irrespective of who occupies central positions in social networks in organizations, the high self-monitors, relative to lows, will be better able to take advantage of the opportunities represented by such positions. High self-monitors, relative to lows, are better at scanning the social world for information about people (Berscheid et al., 1976), the highs are more successful at detecting people's intentions (Jones and Baumeister, 1976), and they are more accurate at eye-witness identification (Hosch et al., 1984). If valuable information is available to those occupying bridging positions in social networks in organizations, then it is more likely to be detected by high self-monitors than by lows.

The third model (the additive model) suggests that the highs are likely to outperform the low self-monitors in ways unrelated to structural position in social networks. Highs are more likely to resolve conflicts through collaboration and compromise (Baron, 1989) and the highs tend to emerge as group leaders (Zaccaro et al., 1991).

Which model of self-monitoring and social networks is true? The only research evidence derives from a study of a small high-tech company (Mehra et al., 2001). The self-monitoring results are summarized in Figure 4.3, illustrating a complex picture of how self-monitoring orientation affects the development of social networks.

As suggested in the mediation model, high self-monitors moved over time into positions in friendship networks that spanned across structural holes whereas low self-monitors tended to remain in more cohesive friendship groups. But the results also showed that high self-monitors, relative to low self-monitors, tended to have larger workflow networks. These two effects of self-monitoring on social networks

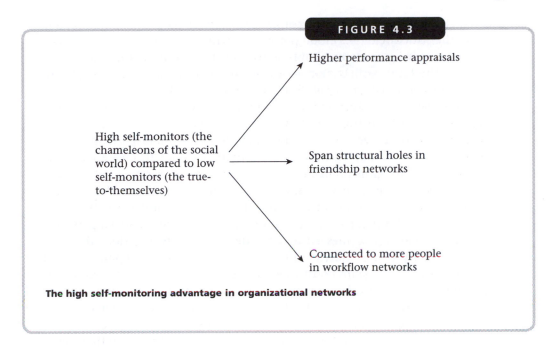

FIGURE 4.3

Higher performance appraisals

High self-monitors (the chameleons of the social world) compared to low self-monitors (the true-to-themselves)

Span structural holes in friendship networks

Connected to more people in workflow networks

The high self-monitoring advantage in organizational networks

had counterbalanced effects on individuals' performance. Whereas centrality in the friendship network helped the high self-monitors' performance, becoming involved in many different projects hurt their performance. Thus, high self-monitors tended to receive higher performance ratings than low self-monitors, but not because of their tendency to occupy central positions in social networks. Overall, centrality in social networks and self-monitoring had independent effects on individuals' performance, supporting a complex additive model of how personality and structural position influenced outcomes.

Important for the present argument was clear evidence that high self-monitors, relative to low self-monitors, did indeed tend to occupy central positions in social networks. Given the overwhelming evidence concerning the stability of self-monitoring orientation, these results are conclusive in showing that personality orientation helps determine the structure of social worlds.

Is there a distinctively structural approach to the question of individual distinctiveness? The answer is yes. Despite more recent dogmatic attempts to exclude individuals and their attributes from network research, we can find traces of a distinctively structural approach to individual differences in the writings of social psychology pioneers such as W.I. Thomas, Georg Simmel, and others, who referred to a concept they termed 'social personality'. Building on such scattered and ambiguous traces, recent work (Oh et al., 2002) has shown that structurally determined social personality is an antecedent of social capital, shaping the structure of ties among business owners.

What is social personality? It was defined rather grandly in the Yankee City studies as 'the total participation of an organic item in its particular part of society' (Warner and Lunt, 1941: 26). Each individual has a distinctive social personality based on that individual's pattern of participation in society. The concept traces its roots back to the work of Simmel (1971) and W.I. Thomas (1927, 1966) concerning the ways in which an individual's participation in society differentiates that individual from others. Individuals create identities for themselves through participation in a range of organizational memberships and activities. In joining an association such as the National Rifle Association, for example, individuals advertise their adherence to typified beliefs, values and actions: an NRA member can be said to have a distinctive social personality. If the individual becomes an officeholder in this organization, then the social personality of the individual becomes clearer. Each individual's set of organizational memberships constitutes an important aspect of individual distinctiveness (Simmel, 1955: 141). The more organizational memberships, the more likely it is that only this individual and no other is differentiated by this particular set of group memberships. In the Yankee City studies, individuals were further differentiated by the levels of prestige they achieved in their set of group memberships. For example, some people become presidents and treasurers of voluntary associations, thereby building their prestige in the community. Thus, key aspects of individual distinctiveness derive from the set of organizations (both voluntary and work organizations) to which the individual belongs, together with the level of prestige the individual achieves in these organizations.

The personality approach to social networks is still in its infancy, but has already shed light on why some individuals tend to transform potential connections into actual connections. All of us have available potential links to others who belong to the sports clubs, alumni associations or religious institutions that we have joined. Some people, more than others, are successful in forging actual links from these potential links. These people tend to be high self-monitors. Further, they tend to be people who have joined many associations, and have gained prestigious positions in these associations. The people who make concrete the virtual connections of joint membership in voluntary associations can be distinguished, therefore, on the basis of their personalities and their social attributes. More research is needed in more bureaucratic organizations, and in organizations with more social divides between groups to determine how self-monitoring combines with network position to affect performance in organizations. Future research could build upon recent contingency approaches to social networks (e.g., Hansen, 1999) to explore different models of how self-monitoring and network position affect performance in different organizational settings. The personality approach may motivate research that helps explain not only why individuals develop distinctive patterns of network ties, but also how these patterns differentially affect outcomes such as work performance, promotions and business success.

It is also possible to imagine that social networks affect those psychological orientations that (unlike self-monitoring) are theorized to be susceptible to radical change. Thus Boissevain (1973) presented some limited evidence suggesting that talkativeness was influenced by whether the individual grew up surrounded by a dense versus a sparse network of neighbourhood connections. There might be similar network effects on such learned dispositions as need for affiliation and need for power (McClelland, 1961). People who find themselves in powerful structural positions in networks may tend to acquire a taste for using such power. It is also possible to imagine that other, more permanent, personality traits (such as the Big Five – Digman, 1990) predispose individuals to create certain types of social network. The reason we have focused on self-monitoring rather than on other personality constructs is that we are able to make clear predictions concerning how self-monitoring orientation affects structural differences in network formation.

SUMMARY

Given the persistence of the anti-categorical imperative among sociological researchers on the one hand (e.g., Mark, 1998) and the neglect of networks by those studying social relations from a psychological perspective on the other hand (e.g., Agnew et al., 2001), there is a pressing need for non-dogmatic research that explores issues concerning how individual differences in cognition and personality relate to the origins and formations of social networks. Drawing on cognitive network theory and emergent personality network theory, we have shown how concepts such as cognitive balance, cognitive accuracy, cognitive maps and self-monitoring help explain how network connections develop, and why individuals' networks in organizations differ. Cognitive network theory and personality theory offer fruitful areas for future social network research. In the next chapter we tackle another neglected topic in social network research on organizations: how organizational networks change over time through processes of goal-directedness and serendipity.

RECOMMENDED FURTHER READING

Kilduff, M. and Krackhardt, D. 1994. Bringing the individual back in: A structural analysis of the internal market for reputation in organizations. *Academy of Management Journal*, 37: 87–108.

Challenges the claimed incommensurability of individualism and structuralism by showing how a cognitive theory guides the use of structural methods. The cognitive theory is balance theory, and the results showed that being perceived to have a prominent friend in an organization boosted individuals' reputations as good performers at work, whereas actually having prominent friends (as assessed by conventional structural methods) had no effect.

Krackhardt, D. and Kilduff, M. 1999. Whether close or far: Social distance effects on perceived balance in friendship networks. *Journal of Personality and Social Psychology*, **76: 770–82.**
Using data from four organizations, the authors investigated balance theory predictions concerning individuals' perceptions of reciprocity and transitivity in friendship relations at work. People tended to perceive relations close to and distant from themselves as more balanced than relations of intermediate distance.

Kumbasar, E.A., Romney, K. and Batchelder, W.H. 1994. Systematic biases in social perception. *American Journal of Sociology*, **100: 477–505.**
For 25 members of one department in a computer company, the authors show that people tend to have biased perceptions of their own positions in friendship networks in the workplace. People see themselves as more central and more popular than is the case. The article is distinguished by its innovative use of correspondence analysis diagrams to portray individuals' network biases visually.

Mayhew, B.H. 1980. Structuralism versus individualism. Part 1: Shadow boxing in the dark. *Social Forces*, **59: 335–75.**
A lively and uncompromising manifesto for the anti-categorical imperative position. Mayhew proclaims the study of individuals to be irrelevant for the purposes of structural analysis. Well worth reading to understand the anti-individualist ideology behind some social network research.

Mehra, A., Kilduff, M. and Brass, D.J. 2001. The social networks of high and low self-monitors: Implications for workplace performance. *Administrative Science Quarterly*, **35: 121–46.**
The first major study of how different personality types create and benefit from social networks in organizations. This study offers an alternative to the standard structuralist assumption that individuals' distinctive dispositions are somehow the residue of their occupation of certain network positions.

5 Network Trajectories: Goal-directed and Serendipitous Processes

How do social networks change over time and what are the implications of network change for individual actors? Even though these questions are of great theoretical and practical interest, organizational network research has tended to neglect issues of network origins and change. The whole panoply of research methods and constructs that make up the network approach militates against consideration of fluidity and transformation in organizational contexts. It is as if network researchers were dazzled by the comments of those foundational writers who suggested that the repetition of behaviour in organizations day after day was so predictable that it could be compared to the repetition of lines 'uttered by Hamlet on the stage' (March and Simon, 1958: 143).

The basic definition of a network as 'a set of nodes and the set of ties' (Brass, 1995: 42) suggests stability. Network relations are the ties that bind, or even, the ties that torture (Krackhardt, 1999). Social networks are analysed in terms of density, hierarchy, multiplexity, interdependence and embeddedness – all terms evocative of the stability of structures of relations. Standard concepts such as structural equivalence seem to imply stability in the roles that actors occupy in social space. As one book chapter has put the situation: 'Enormous research remains to be done in the dynamics of social networks' (Degenne and Forse, 1999: 159).

To the extent that network researchers have investigated network change processes within organizational settings, the tendency has been to model simulated relationships while calling for more of the realistic details necessary 'to develop even a relatively simple computational model' (Carley, 1999). We aim to offer an overarching theory of network change that can facilitate research into both simulated and actual network dynamics. At the interorganizational level, we do know that relationships are more likely to occur between organizations that are interdependent and that have a prior history of relationships (Gulati and Gargiulo, 1999). Further, ties between organizations tend to be embedded in personal relationships between the managers and owners of those organizations. As one pioneering analysis of collaboration between high-growth firms stated: 'Personal reputations, as well as histories and individual friendships, were important factors in explaining the formation of ties' (Larson, 1992: 84). Another excellent study of organizational networks provided evidence that new ties between organizations were arranged through interpersonal contacts. A typical process would be for business owner A to ask business owner B (a close friend) to form a tie with business owner C (another close friend) (Uzzi, 1996: 679). Thus, to some extent, the macro-level processes of tie formation between organizations reflect the micro-level processes of interpersonal trust formation between individuals. We build on that insight in our theory development.

In our approach to network change, we introduce the concept of a network trajectory. This allows us to move back and forth between the micro and the macro as we consider the sequence of changes that each trajectory entails in internal identity and external relationships (see Goffman, 1961: 128–9). Our approach operates at a relatively high level of theoretical abstraction. We offer an ideal type perspective, focusing on two distinctly different change processes (goal-directed and serendipitous). We endeavour to provide a two-sided consideration of change, incorporating both the relationship of the network to other social institutions (such as formal organizations) and the relationship of the network to its members.

GOAL-DIRECTEDNESS AND SERENDIPITY

In considering network trajectories, we distinguish between two processes: goal-directedness and serendipity. These two processes produce quite different network trajectories. Further, these two processes differ fundamentally in operation and structural dynamics. As one of our shrewdest organizational theorists commented in his call for a better theory of network change, some network processes involved interaction 'to achieve, plan, coordinate, or decide on … individual and collective activities' whereas other network processes involve 'the happenstance of people meeting and liking one another' (Salancik, 1995: 346). Goal-directed and serendipitous processes are ideal types that allow us to differentiate between two different trajectories over time.

Goal-directed Network Trajectories

Examples of network change driven primarily by goal-directedness include the trajectories of certain types of multilateral networks of cooperating firms as well as the trajectories of networking clubs. In multilateral cooperating firm networks with clear goals, member firms are reported to 'see themselves as part of the network and are committed to network-level goals' (Human and Provan, 2000: 329). For example, a wood-industry manufacturing network founded in 1989 by a core group of ten firms quickly expanded to 60 firms when the goals of the network were clarified to include tangible benefits to members such as exhibition space for wood products in a combination showroom gallery. When the showroom was unexpectedly closed for a year, the network lost some of its goal-directed focus and membership dropped by half (Human and Provan, 2000: 334–5). Goal-directed network dynamics are sensitive to the articulation and coherence of network-level goals.

One of the key identifying features of goal-directedness in network change is the emergence of an administrative entity that acts as a broker to plan and coordinate the activities of the network as a whole. This entity can be a member of the network itself or a separate actor with a specialized coordinating role: 'It is the role of this entity to help build the network, coordinate and manage its activities, support network firms and network-level goals, and provide a centralized location for performing key activities of the network' (Human and Provan, 2000: 329).

Goal-directed network trajectories develop around specific goals that members share. For example, a regional business network might organize around the goal of promoting member interaction and joint marketing. All the relationships among business organizations in the network would be mobilized to achieve this goal. Similarly, a job-getting network might be organized to help all the members in the network find jobs. All the relationships among individuals in the network would be structured to achieve the goal.

Serendipitous Network Trajectories

When network change is driven primarily by serendipity, network trajectories develop haphazardly from the interactions of individual actors. There are no network-level goals to drive the process of interaction. At any point in time, any specific pair of actors may or may not share goals. At the interorganizational level, some interlocking directorate networks follow serendipitous trajectories. Two firms may forge a tie in such a network if a director of one firm accepts the offer of a board seat on another firm. In some cases each of the two firms that are joined may have a strategic interest in the other's activities. A bank, for example, may place a director on the board a firm to which it has loaned money. Both the bank and the indebted firm in such a case are likely to share the goal of promoting the firm's financial well-being. In other cases, two firms may share nothing except the coincidence of having the same person sit on their boards.

At the individual-person level, many interpersonal networks follow serendipitous paths. Each individual in the network may pursue friendship or interaction with one or more others but, at any point in time, any two randomly chosen members of the network are unlikely to share any network-level goals and may not be friendly or interactive with each other.

The small-world phenomenon illustrates the surprising prevalence of serendipity as an organizing principle in creating relatively invisible chains of connections that help knit society together. Recent estimates suggest that in modern societies, each adult has about 5,000 acquaintances, of which 100–200 could be contacted immediately in order to expedite a request. Only about 20 people count as regular interlocutors, however, and of these 20, confidants number about three (Degenne and Forse, 1999: 21). Thus, surrounding each person like an invisible nimbus is a vast circle of relationships that connect the person, through ever-widening circles of friends of friends, and acquaintances of acquaintances, to practically everyone else on the planet. Research suggests that between any two people in the USA there are about five or six links (Travers and Milgram, 1969).

In serendipitous network processes, individual actors make choices about who to connect with, what to transact, and so on, without guidance from any central network agent concerning goals or strategy. Actors form ties or partnerships based on their own interests. Serendipitous networking can provide conduits through which information and other resources flow. In theory, goal-directedness and serendipity can produce quite different network trajectories. We recognize that goal-directed and serendipitous processes are ideal types and that many actual network trajectories exhibit both processes. Nevertheless, the analytical distinction between the two types enables us, we believe, to make progress on Salancik's (1995) demand for a good network theory of organization. In this section, we contrast two ideal-type trajectories, one driven primarily by goal-directedness and the other driven primarily by serendipity. These two trajectories differ in terms of several characteristics, including underlying assumptions, stages of growth, structural dynamics, implications for individual actors, and patterns of migration and transformation. We summarize the major differences in Table 5.1.

TABLE 5.1

Goal-directed versus serendipitous processes in networks

	Goal-directed process dominant	Serendipitous process dominant
Underlying assumptions	Teleological and instrumental. Actors share a goal. Network is formed to achieve this goal. Success is measured against this goal.	No pre-existent goal. Network evolves through random variation, selection and retention process.
Typical network growth	Fast to form around shared goals. Survival threatened by both success and failure. New goal discovery prolongs life span.	Slower to form. Grows through dyadic ties. Long-lived, robust survival in times of change.
Structural dynamics	Centralized structure with a leader: core-periphery. Minimizes structural holes. Tight coupling. Clear boundary. Growth based on eligibility. Less likely to survive sub-network formation.	Decentralized structure with no single leader. Produces structural holes. Loose coupling. Diffuse boundary. Growth based on dyadic match. More likely to create sub-networks, over time.
Conflict	If conflicts arise over goals, probable break-up of network.	Sub-groups, each with internal solidarity, can survive in the same network.
Implications for individual actors	More homogeneous actors. Actors participate based on shared goals. Mobility across similar organizations. More predictable career path. Emphasis on network-wide trust.	More diverse actors. Actors participate based on shared ties. Mobility through network links. Unexpected career change may occur. Emphasis on interpersonal trust at dyadic level.

UNDERLYING ASSUMPTIONS

The two network trajectories both incorporate the full range of network relations given that both goal-directed and serendipitous network processes affect friendship relations advice relations, and exchange. These processes can therefore drive the development of both expressive and instrumental networks in organizations (see Lincoln and Miller, 1979). The difference between the two network trajectories has to do with the presence or absence of teleology. One trajectory (the goal-directed) is driven forward towards the accomplishment of goals, whereas the other trajectory (the serendipitous) capitalizes on opportunism in the absence of overarching goals. In organizational contexts, social support and other expressive networks are sometimes organized centrally, supported by the organization, and devoted to promoting employee development and commitment (see Friedman, 1996). Instrumental networks such as advice often develop haphazardly around local leaders who manage constituencies without any central authority or even knowledge by management (see Burt and Ronchi, 1990).

The goal-directed network trajectory exhibits purposive and adaptive movement towards an envisioned end state (Van de Ven and Poole, 1995: 516). A network energized by such a goal has a purpose that enables it to organize its members, facilitate meetings and pursue resources. New members are attracted to the network by the promise of goal-fulfilment, so there is a pre-selection process that screens possible members on the basis of fit with the goals of the existing network.

So-called 'networking clubs' have proliferated in recent years in order to help members make contacts and referrals. The typical activity of such a club has been described as follows: 'Every member is *required* to make an average of two referrals a week. … When you join a networking club, you immediately get a new set of *direct* contacts. … But it's the *indirect* contacts that really make a difference' (Baker, 1994: 265). These clubs vary enormously in terms of focus but, according to Baker (1994: 267), the majority 'are devoted to career development and job hunting'. The best clubs are those that have a specific goal. These networks are driven forward by specific goals.

A network that follows a serendipitous development path has no pre-existing goal around which members cluster. The organizing principle is not goal consensus but dyadic matching in an evolutionary process of random variation, selection and retention. Potential members may bump into each other because of accidents of geography or schedule. From these multiple dyadic encounters, some connections are made based on homophily of attributes or interests, and some of these connections endure.

Serendipitous networking capitalizes on opportunity. For example, the directors of Acme Corporation may or may not decide to take advantage of offers to join the boards of other corporations. If the directors do join other boards, then ties are formed between Acme and other corporations through the opportunism of directors. It is in this sense that networks change through processes that at the level of the network have no overall goal. Serendipitous networking relies on processes of chance and opportunism, whereas goal-directed networking relies on purposiveness.

An example of how a serendipitous network trajectory develops was provided in the study of veterans' housing at Massachusetts Institute of Technology. Second World War veterans commencing their studies at MIT were allocated housing and found themselves by chance inhabiting units next to neighbours with whom they had no previous acquaintance. What happened in the absence of any organizing goal concerning whom to seek out for friendly interaction? 'People who lived close to one another became friendly with each other, while people who lived far apart did not. Mere "accidents" of where a path went or whose doorway a staircase passed were major determinants of who became friends within this community' (Festinger et al., 1950: 10). Connections developed not through any goal orientation or overall organizing process, but through the happenstance of individual interaction. In this case, opportunism took advantage of residential proximity. In other cases, accidents of timing or market inefficiencies can lead actors to establish ties to those with whom they happen to come into contact.

NETWORK TRAJECTORIES OVER TIME

The goal-directed network trajectory starts with the establishment of a goal. In the case of a group of the recently unemployed, this might be the goal of helping members get jobs. The next stage is typically to set up a meeting at which organizing principles are established. These principles might include the dues members are expected to contribute, the frequency and place of meetings, the officers, if any, that are to run the network, and the basic agenda the network will pursue. The third stage is often the search for outside resources to supplement those that exist within the network. In the case of a job search network, outside resources could include grants from ex-employers or city agencies either in cash or in kind (use of office space, for example). The fourth stage is the assessment of progress towards the goal: Have the members succeeded in getting jobs? If the network fails in meeting its goal (nobody finds a job after two years), then its demise may be swift. Similarly, if the goal is met (everyone finds a job within six months), the network may cease to exist. But the network may also invent a new goal – to help members get promotions, for example. This would then start the process of network change all over again.

Goal-directed network trajectories can differ depending on initial conditions and other factors. A comparative study of two networks of wood-product manufacturers (Alpha-net and Beta-net) showed that both networks were formed to promote joint marketing, production and development activities; and both networks established central entities with executive directors (Human and Provan, 2000). In the case of Alpha-net, an entrepreneurial broker initially brought the ten original firms together in a conference and this broker was then hired as director of the putative network's central coordinating entity. In contrast, for Beta-net the central entity and its director were funded by a state agency to recruit network members. Both Alpha-net and Beta-net promoted new friendships among participants from different firms, as well as business and informational exchange, through monthly membership and board meetings. Funding at Alpha-net first came from member dues, but by the second year Alpha-net had acquired a substantial government grant. Beta-net's original focus on outside funding was reflected in its networking activity aimed at outside funding organizations. When external funding dried up in the second year, Beta-net ceased to exist. Thus, the trajectories of these two networks were similar in the phases they moved through, but were also sensitive to differences in initial conditions, differences that became amplified in terms of how the network organized its members and interacted with the environment.

Serendipitous network trajectories, despite the absence of network-wide development strategies, also exhibit predictable patterns of change. A network that relies on serendipity starts as individual actors in social contexts such as organizations act independently to establish ties to others. An interpersonal friendship network, for example, can begin with one individual signalling friendliness to another. The second stage involves reciprocity: the process of reciprocity ensures that a tie offered by one party tends to be returned. Reciprocity is a basic operating principle of sentiment-based relations and other types of relations (Gouldner, 1960) and tends to appear relatively quickly in the life-cycle of the emerging network system (Doreian, 2002). The third stage involves transitivity. An actor who has two friends in common will tend to bring the two friends together so that three dyads are joined in what Krackhardt (1999) has termed a Simmelian triad. This triad tends to be very stable, and to exert pressure on the members of the dyads to conform to an overarching set of assumptions and constraints at the triad level. The fourth stage is the clustering together of triads and dyads into structures that graph theorists refer to as components – dense areas in which all actors are connected to one or more of the other actors and no actors have connections outside the component (Wasserman and Faust, 1994: 109–10). The fifth stage involves the emergence of brokers who span across clusters, enabling information and other resources to move around the network. Eventually the serendipitous process may approach a situation of quasi-balance in which two or more large components have developed, each component characterized by an emergent but diffuse set of cultural expectations concerning attitudes and behaviour.

Thus the serendipitous network trajectory evolves through a predictable process of clustering and bridging as individual actors make choices based on dyadic attraction. The goal-directed network trajectory, in contrast, is driven forwards through phases of development by the pursuit of a goal. Note that processes of reciprocity and transitivity, which are basic features of human interaction, show up in all social network development. The difference is that goal-directed networking provides members with a shared object of positive regard (the goal). Goal-directed networking dynamics are compatible with the original formulation of balance theory in which actors are hypothesized to like each other if they have joint ties to objects that can be psychological or physical entities (Heider, 1958). Processes of friendship formation and reciprocity at the network level are considerably accelerated when all actors share positive regard for network goals and concomitant activities.

STRUCTURAL DYNAMICS

The network that pursues a goal-directed trajectory is from the beginning highly structured around a leader or set of leaders who articulate the goals of the putative organization and recruit members. Attempts to avoid network hierarchy in the name of egalitarianism are likely to founder over the course of the network trajectory as the network consolidates around goal-directed leadership (Michels, 1962). The network is therefore likely to exhibit a centre–periphery structure, and to grow from the centre outwards, adding more members at the periphery. The common goals, scheduled meetings and clear agenda are likely to build strong bonds of generalized trust among those members at the centre of the network. These members are likely to be connected not just to one or two other members but to many other members, leading to a tightly-coupled central structure in which, for example, a defection by one member may affect the whole of the central core.

Goal-directedness establishes a clear boundary that differentiates between members and non-members. Eligibility rules are also likely to be clear and may be imposed in a formal vetting process applied to potential recruits to the network. Member benefits and obligations are likely to be well defined and may even be written down. Thus goal-directed networking tends to invoke features of a bureaucracy. The act of joining a network organized around specific goals is likely to be a momentous one for many of the individual participants. For example, one such network limited its membership to 45, with any new applicant rejected if even one existing member objected. The network required members to meet every Thursday evening for a set format that included two 15-minute presentations. Members contributed mandatory dues, active participation was required, attendance was recorded, and statistics of member referrals were compiled every month (Baker, 1994: 269).

The explicit controls and incentives concerning member participation indicate a general problem for networks that pursue goals – a tendency for a boundary to develop within the network between active and passive members. The active members may tend to cluster around the central core, attend meetings, debate policy and pursue goal accomplishment. The passive members may tend to be little more than names on the membership rolls, recipients of newsletters and payers of dues (Human and Provan, 2000). Thus structural holes between components are unlikely to develop over the course of goal-directed network trajectories. Instead, the structural divide is likely to be between an active connected group at the centre and a passive disaggregated group scattered around the periphery.

The centralization that accompanies goal-directedness is likely to be exhibited in such features as common pooling of resources, election of officers, and centralized contact between the network and outside bodies. The emergence of a clear boundary, centralized leadership and tight coupling between members can permit a network to represent itself as an actor in political and other arenas. Goal-directedness will drive the network, over time, to resemble a formal organization, albeit one that continues to depend on voluntary activities and reciprocated helping.

To the extent that a network relies on serendipitous processes of member interaction, it is likely to have no centralized core of members. Instead, clusters of members are likely to grow by a process of dyadic attraction: an existing member of the network is likely to form an attachment to an outside member who then is joined to the network. The members of the network are likely to have no clear picture of network structure or membership given that the network exists as an analytical description rather than as purposeful entity. Meetings between members are likely to be strictly local affairs rather than organized network events. Strong bonds of trust are likely to be formed between locally connected members. The overall structure of the network is therefore likely to be loosely coupled. The addition or loss of members will have relatively little effect on the network as a whole. Most members of the network are likely to be connected to only a small proportion of the overall network. The act of joining this loosely-coupled network may have little effect on many new members.

Serendipitous network trajectories are likely to produce poorly-defined boundaries, although any network can be arbitrarily restricted, for the purpose of analysis, to the set of members that interact within some specific geographic location (such as an organization) or social context (such as boards of directors). Given that members are recruited on the basis of serendipitous encounters, eligibility rules are often quite general (e.g., existence of a friendship tie to an existing member), and member benefits and responsibilities are generally either unclear or tacit. Ties between members are often strong (e.g., friendship ties) but across the network there will be many weak ties between people who know of each other (friends of friends) but who rarely interact (see Kadushin, 1966, on social circles).

Thus serendipitous network trajectories will tend to continually produce structural holes (or quasi structural holes) between clusters that have no ties (or few ties). The active members of the network will tend to be the brokers who span across the network, providing information and links from one part of the loosely-coupled network to another part. Other active leaders may emerge within clusters as representatives of specific interest groups or cabals. As structural holes are bridged by network entrepreneurs, new holes are likely to emerge from the constant process of member addition and subtraction as people ally with and depart from the network. Evidence suggests that structural holes in organizational settings tend to vanish with remarkable rapidity (Burt, 2002).

The decentralization that accompanies serendipitous networking will show up, therefore, in the existence of multiple dense regions within which members have many ties to each other. These multiple centres will tend to be bridged by brokerage ties in a dynamic process that resembles two sets of crystalline structures reaching towards each other on a frozen window-pane. Serendipitous networking, with its absence of bureaucracy, offers network entrepreneurs opportunities to play leading roles in knowledge flow.

Conflict

In goal-directed networking processes, the potential for conflict is likely to arise when goals are being established and when goal accomplishment is being assessed. A dominant coalition may impose a goal, and recruit on the basis of that goal, but face a group of actors who interact around a competing goal. If goals are the organizing principle of network development, goal conflict can be costly and, if not resolved, can lead directly to the break-up of the network into two different networks or to the abandonment of the network.

A network that has been driven forward in the pursuit of a goal will, in the presence of goal-conflict, tend to form two groups differentiated on the basis of different goals. Each group is likely to exhibit a hierarchical structure, so that the network as a whole will display two centres of power. One example of this is provided by a karate club before and after its split into two different clubs (see Zachary, 1977 for a detailed description). There was an ideological conflict between the club president and the club instructor over both the price of karate lessons and the type of karate being practised. As time passed the entire karate club became divided over these issues. Figure 5.1 illustrates the split of the network not just into two groups but into two hierarchically organized groups. Part (a) shows the extent to which the karate club, prior to the break-up, was differentiated into two blocks. Part(b) shows the extent to which the rival factions organized around the two leaders – the club president (number 34) and Mr Hi, the instructor (number 1). Because of the existence of two factions with different goals, this goal-oriented network became unstable and broke into two separate clubs, each with a different karate orientation. Figure 5.1(c) shows the characteristic core–periphery structure of the two new goal-directed networks. The centralization indices for the new networks are high, indicating the high degree of centralization around the leaders.

The serendipitous network trajectory develops, as we have said, through processes of local balance between interacting actors. Ties accumulate as reciprocity develops between dyads and as transitivity develops among triads. This progression is likely to feature a growing likelihood of schism between cohesive sub-groups, although these groups are unlikely to be hierarchically organized.

FIGURE 5.1A

(a) Blocked matrix

```
                      1 1 1 1 1 1 2 2   1     1 1 2 1 2 2 2 2 2 2 2 3 3 3 3 3
            1 2 3 4 5 6 7 8 7 8 1 2 3 4 0 2   5 9 9 6 1 0 3 4 5 6 7 8 9 0 1 2 3 4
   1   1 | 1 1 1 1 1 1 1   1 1 1 1 1 1 1 | 1                             1        |
   2   2 | 1   1 1       1   1       1 1 1 |                         1              |
   3   3 | 1 1   1       1           1     | 1         1         1 1         1     |
   4   4 | 1 1 1         1         1 1     |                                       |
   5   5 | 1           1       1           |                                       |
   6   6 | 1           1   1   1           |                                       |
   7   7 | 1       1 1       1             |                                       |
   8   8 | 1 1 1 1                         |                                       |
  17  17 |             1 1                 |                                       |
  18  18 | 1 1                             |                                       |
  11  11 | 1         1 1                   |                                       |
  12  12 | 1                               |                                 1     |
  13  13 | 1       1                       |                                 1     |
  14  14 | 1 1 1 1                         |                                       |
  20  20 | 1 1                             |                                       |
  22  22 | 1 1                             |                                       |
        +- - - - - - - - - - - - - - - - -+- - - - - - - - - - - - - - - - - - - -+
  15  15 |                                 |                                   1 1 |
   9   9 | 1   1                           |                         1         1 1 |
  19  19 |                                 |                                   1 1 |
  16  16 |                                 |                                   1 1 |
  21  21 |                                 |                                   1 1 |
  10  10 |       1                         |                                     1 |
  23  23 |                                 |                                   1 1 |
  24  24 |                                 |                 1   1   1       1 1 |
  25  25 |                                 |                 1   1       1         |
  26  26 |                                 |             1 1             1         |
  27  27 |                                 |                         1       1     |
  28  28 |       1                         |                 1 1             1     |
  29  29 |       1                         |                             1   1     |
  30  30 |                                 |                 1   1           1 1 |
  31  31 |   1                             | 1                                 1 1 |
  32  32 | 1                               |                 1 1     1         1 1 |
  33  33 |       1                         | 1 1 1 1 1   1 1         1 1 1     1   |
  34  34 |                         1 1     | 1 1 1 1 1 1 1 1   1 1 1 1 1 1 1       |
        +- - - - - - - - - - - - - - - - -+- - - - - - - - - - - - - - - - - - - -+
```

The so-called balance theorem states that 'if balance theory processes are operative, the resulting structure is a group where there are two mutually hostile subgroups each with internal solidarity' (Doreian, 2002: 97). Thus, networks that follow a serendipitous trajectory have an internal mechanism of conflict that, over time, is likely to lead to the survival within the network of two distinct groups, each with its own loosely-defined cultural consensus.

FIGURE 5.1B,C

(b) Sociogram of karate club members' interactions

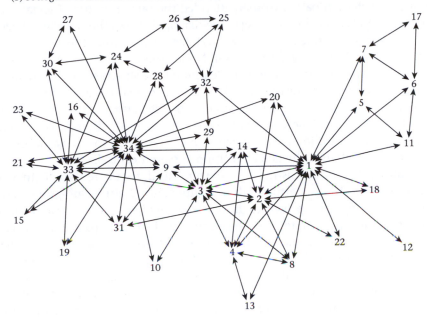

(c) Break-up of club into two separatae karate clubs

Officer's Karate Club

Mr Hi's Karate Club

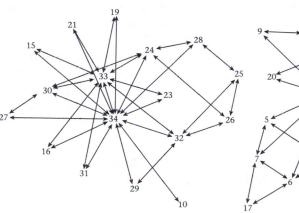
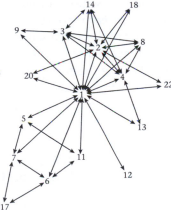

Officers' Club = 72.5%   Degree centralization   Hi's Club = 77.1%

Goal-directed processes and structure in the karate network

One example of serendipitous processes producing the characteristic pattern of two sub-groups within the same network is provided in the different parts of Figure 5.2. This is the famous southern women data set. Figure 5.2(a) shows the extent to which each pair of women attended the same number of social events (as recorded in the local newspaper). The diagonal shows the number of events that each woman attended. Figure 5.2(b) is taken directly from the original report of this network (Davis et al., 1941: 150). Notice that, despite myths to the contrary, the original authors had no trouble finding the structure in these data, and putting the women into distinct blocks. Figure 5.2(c) shows a sociogram of the whole network based on the decision to record a tie between any pair of women who attended three or more of the same social events. If the rule is relaxed to allow a tie to occur for joint attendance at one event, then the network becomes even more characteristically dense, with no apparent centralization.

As all writers about this network have noticed, there are two distinct sub-groups, as shown in the bottom half of Figure 5.2(c). Neither sub-group is hier-archical. Serendipitous processes have established instead cohesion among members. Unlike the karate club, the existence of sub-groups did not threaten the survival of the network, and there were network entrepreneurs (visible in the picture of the complete network) who bridged across the social divides.

Networks that develop through serendipity can exist as latent structures, relatively invisible because they lack the trappings of bureaucracy. Such networks have no offices or officers. Leaders, to the extent that they exist, tend to be informal. We should not make the mistake, however, of believing that such a loosely-organized network lacks power to frustrate or facilitate activity. The network can be activated by conflict with bureaucracy in a way that can seem baffling to those blind to serendipity's relatively invisible functioning. In one case, a CEO was frightened by a series of events that included the failure of projects originating in his office, the leaking of sensitive discussions with senior management, threats of violence received by himself and his family, together with expressions of hatred from employees. These were all symptoms of a social network that had been activated following the firing of a man who, over the course of 30 years, had, like many other employees, attracted friends and family to the manufacturing facility in a process that was invisible to management (Burt and Ronchi, 1990).

IMPLICATIONS OF NETWORK TRAJECTORIES FOR INDIVIDUAL ACTORS

If we consider the two types of network process as organizational-level pheno-mena that affect network development over time, the question arises as to what the implications are for employees of organizations. An example of a network of organizations joined by a common goal is a group of business schools

FIGURE 5.2

(a) Similarity matrix showing number of activities southern women attended together

		1	2	3	4	5	6	7	8	9	1 0	1 1	1 2	1 3	1 4	1 5	1 6	1 7	1 8
		E	L	T	B	C	F	E	P	R	V	M	K	S	N	H	D	O	F
1	EVELYN	8	6	7	6	3	4	3	3	3	2	2	2	2	2	1	2	1	1
2	LAURA	6	7	6	6	3	4	4	2	3	2	1	1	2	2	2	1	0	0
3	THERESA	7	6	8	6	4	4	4	3	4	3	2	2	3	3	2	2	1	1
4	BRENDA	6	6	6	7	4	4	4	2	3	2	1	1	2	2	2	1	0	0
5	CHARLOTTE	3	3	4	4	4	2	2	0	2	1	0	0	1	1	1	0	0	0
6	FRANCES	4	4	4	4	2	4	3	2	2	1	1	1	1	1	1	1	0	0
7	ELEANOR	3	4	4	4	2	3	4	2	3	2	1	1	2	2	2	1	0	0
8	PEARL	3	2	3	2	0	2	2	3	2	2	2	2	2	2	1	2	1	1
9	RUTH	3	3	4	3	2	2	3	2	4	3	2	2	3	2	2	2	1	1
10	VERNE	2	2	3	2	1	1	2	2	3	4	3	3	4	3	3	3	1	1
11	MYRNA	2	1	2	1	0	1	1	2	2	3	4	4	4	3	3	4	1	1
12	KATHERINE	2	1	2	1	0	1	1	2	2	3	4	6	6	5	5	4	1	1
13	SYLVIA	2	2	3	2	1	1	2	2	3	4	4	6	7	6	6	4	1	1
14	NORA	2	2	3	2	1	1	2	2	3	3	3	5	6	8	6	3	2	2
15	HELEN	1	2	2	2	1	1	2	1	2	3	3	5	6	6	7	3	1	1
16	DOROTHY	2	1	2	1	0	1	1	2	2	3	4	4	4	3	3	4	1	1
17	OLIVIA	1	0	1	0	0	0	0	1	1	1	1	1	1	2	1	1	2	2
18	FLORA	1	0	1	0	0	0	0	1	1	1	1	1	1	2	1	1	2	2

(b) Blocked matrix

								Events							
		1	2	3	4	5	6	7	8	9	10	11	12	13	14
1	EVELYN	1	1	1	1	1	1		1	1					
2	LAURA	1	1	1		1	1	1	1						
3	THERESA		1	1	1	1	1	1	1	1					
4	BRENDA	1		1	1	1	1	1	1						
5	CHARLOTTE			1	1	1		1							
6	FRANCES			1		1	1		1						
7	ELEANOR					1	1	1	1						
8	PEARL						1		1	1					
9	RUTH					1		1	1	1					
10	VERNE							1	1	1		1			
11	MYRNA							1	1	1	1	1			
12	KATHERINE							1	1	1	1		1	1	1
13	SYLVIA							1	1	1	1		1	1	1
14	NORA					1	1		1	1	1	1	1	1	1
15	HELEN							1	1		1	1	1	1	1
16	DOROTHY							1	1	1	1				
17	OLIVIA								1		1				
18	FLORA								1		1				

FIGURE 5.2C

(c) Sociograms of southern women activity network

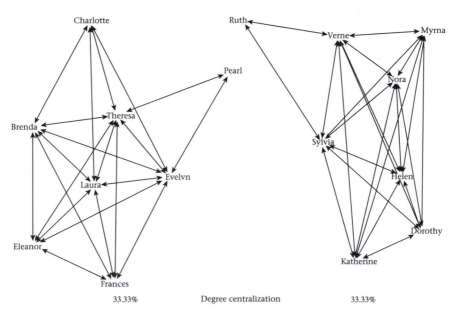

Degree centralization = 34.6%

33.33%   Degree centralization   33.33%

Serendipity processes and structure in southern women activities

that have chosen each other after careful deliberation as partners in research and student exchange. An example of a network of organizations joined by serendipity is a group of business schools linked by haphazard bilateral agreements set up on a dyadic basis by individual deans and other decision-makers – the network as a whole would not be aware of its own existence.

Goal-directedness attracts to the network organizations that share the same goals. These networks tend, therefore, to become relatively homogeneous. For example, a regional industrial network of small producers will tend to attract companies that face the same environments and problems, hire similar people and function in similar ways. Employees of such organizations are likely to benefit from contact with their peers in other organizations in terms of social comparisons concerning pay and other opportunities. If there are disparities between the pay and benefits of one organization and another within the network, there is likely to be pressure for equity to be established. Regular meetings between the representatives of the member organizations are likely to diffuse best practices and opportunities throughout the network.

There is also the possibility of cross-organizational career moves that become facilitated as a result of individuals' greater familiarity with professionals in the same region and industry. People meet each other in arenas of mutual support and striving at network events, and this promotes a generalized trust within the whole network. Individuals may come to think of themselves as network members, thereby adding to their personal identities a connection to the network-level goals. When leadership positions become available in one of the networked organizations, there is likely to be at least a consideration of available individuals from within the set of organizations in the network. Thus, the labour market for talent is likely to expand to include employees of all the organizations active in pursuit of network goals.

Further, the increased contact that the network offers with outside organizations may enable individuals to gain contacts that can enhance career options. To the extent, for example, that network representatives interact with government organizations, foundations or other establishments, career opportunities are likely to increase outside the network. As a result of contacts with other networks or establishments, information may flow into the network concerning personnel practices in other parts of the country and the world. This information can radically change the taken-for-granted routines within firms, either enhancing or destroying the competencies of organizational personnel. To the extent that network activity reduces isolation and promotes innovation, there are likely to be winners and losers among the personnel in the participating firms. Careers can be enhanced for those who champion new trends that appear to promote competitiveness.

The interlocking directorate network is one example of a relatively serendipitous firm-level networking. At the network level there may be no specific goal that unites all the members of the network. Career benefits from network ties are likely to flow to local parts of the overall network rather than be diffused across the whole network. For example, the career of an executive who sits on other boards can benefit directly from these personal ties. The executive is likely to become more experienced at high-level policy decision-making, and become visible outside his or her employing organization. When vacancies occur at the highest level, the names of such well-connected executives are likely to be well-known. Their cross-organizational mobility is likely to be enhanced not just within the industry, but also outside the industry, given their expertise at the highest managerial levels of board activity.

The utility of weak ties has been much discussed since Granovetter's (1973) initial formulation. The weak-tie hypothesis implies that the benefits to members of networks flow not just to those who have strong ties (i.e., to the people who occupy seats on other firms' boards), but are also available to those who have contact with these interlocking board members. Given the notorious inefficiency of labour markets, people who hear about potential vacancies and opportunities are likely to have a considerable advantage in the race to move ahead in the corporate world. Serendipitous networking is likely to channel information and other benefits to strategically well-placed firms, and employees within those firms. Unlike goal-directed networking, there is unlikely to be a central distribution of resources throughout the network.

EGOCENTRIC NETWORKS

Serendipitous and goal-directed processes change networks over time. Paralleling these changes are changes in the networks of individual actors. There is a co-evolution of network trajectories and individual actors' networks. Actors (whether individual people or organizations) influence and are influenced by social network trajectories. Actors add and subtract connections to networks as they make or break dyadic links, trailing their own egocentric networks with them. Through this process of actor engagement and disengagement, connections and disconnections are made to a range of other bounded groups. So both actors and the networks to which they belong move through a successive series of states, with decisions being made at the actor level affecting network-level outcomes, whereas network evolution facilitates and constrains actors' networking.

At the individual level the person pursues a career through a succession of organizations that include the family, the school, voluntary associations (such as churches and sports clubs), college and work. Notice that many of these network connections are involuntary on the part of individuals. No one chooses which family to be born into or which school to attend. Similarly, the choice of a house of worship is a decision usually taken on behalf of the individual by the family and the community within which the individual child is embedded. So, many network connections that have profound influence on the individual's egocentric network development are already in place before the age of deliberate choice. The individual may be conscious of choosing to invite one friend rather than another home to play, but even these choices, for young children, are subject to parental negotiation and approval. Network connections that can influence future opinions, actions and the trajectories of social networks are already in place for individuals as they reach adulthood. Organizational memberships in schools, clubs, voluntary associations, churches, etc., have been taken with little or no input from the individual. The apparently voluntarily chosen egocentric networks are therefore largely predetermined for individuals as they reach adulthood.

For individuals born into social circles of privilege and status, serendipitous networking among people they encounter socially can provide the contacts that help entry into exclusive schools, clubs and jobs. Research shows that having contacts in a company helps people gain jobs (Fernandez and Weinberg, 1997) and negotiate higher salaries at the time of job entry (Seidel et al., 2000). For people born into social circles of deprivation and low status, serendipitous networking is unlikely to facilitate contacts that bridge across social divides. Goal-directed networking that targets individuals who move in circles different from those into which the individual finds himself or herself is more likely to provide access to important information, resources and further contacts.

Given the bounded set of network memberships available to individuals, choices can, however, allow individuals to represent themselves as unique personalities in the social world. As Georg Simmel wrote, memberships in different social circles 'give an individual of many gifts the opportunity to pursue each of his interests in association with others' (Simmel, 1955: 162). Each individual's set of memberships in networks helps establish the individual as a distinctive person. Network memberships provide a basis for individuals to develop distinctive egocentric network trajectories through intensive interaction with bounded webs of affiliation characteristic of associations and formal organizations.

The individual seldom arrives at a new context shorn of previous organizational commitments that may facilitate or hinder adaptation to a new set of network patterns. Goal-directed networking can drastically expand the range of connections available to an individual. Such efforts can facilitate the radical transformation of egocentric networks. Similarly, individuals who cultivate serendipitous encounters can promote the possibility that chance connections can lead their egocentric networks in quite new directions.

The process of getting a job is famously dependent on the structure of weak ties that individuals have accumulated in their progress through different social spheres (Granovetter, 1973). The path-dependent characteristic of egocentric network trajectories is evident in the finding that members of some demographic groups find themselves disadvantaged with respect to the ties that facilitate not only job offers but also higher starting salaries (Seidel et al., 2000). Not all network trajectories are equal – some people bring more diverse and useful sets of connections with them as they move through the contemporary landscape of organizational settings.

An individual who wished to change completely the trajectory of his or her egocentric network would have to forswear childhood friends, faith or mentors in pursuit of a completely different future. Some organizational cults appear to have specialized in creating new network trajectories for people who fall under their influence, systematically cutting recruits off from contact with previous networks, and this kind of radical re-engineering of egocentric networks has long been the practice of total institutions (Goffman, 1961).

NETWORK MIGRATION AND TRANSFORMATION

So far we have kept the two types of network process separate, treating goal-directedness and serendipity as though each was quite distinct from the other. We have further assumed that each network trajectory could develop separately, but this is only one of four possible scenarios. We must also recognize that one trajectory could colonize the other, so that a network developing through a serendipitous process could become partly or completely goal-directed and vice versa. We consider these possibilities below.

Each Network Process Develops Independently

Since Weber, organizational theory has warned against an admixture of informal relations in formal settings. Some networks are likely to hold fast to shared goals and are likely to avoid haphazard recruitment on the basis of kinship or friendship. In such a network, actors are likely to emphasize goal achievement, and recognize that the network has a single goal that does not impinge on other areas of activity. For example, a running network might involve people who meet at lunchtime to run, but otherwise never interact with each other. One of the explicit rules of membership might be to keep personal and professional matters quite separate from the network's goals that revolve around shared running and fitness development.

The maintenance of goal-directedness might require a vigilant focus on the instrumental use of social ties, and a willingness to refuse membership to some and to cancel membership of others. There may be a clear trajectory of tie-cutting and adding in pursuit of goals. Goal-directedness requires a great deal of explicit management in order to ensure resources are being used for goal accomplishment. Ties that were once useful but are no longer tolerable are likely to be bought off or simply cut. Otherwise actors are likely to use the network for purposes such as mere socializing.

Are there pure examples of goal-directed networks in which serendipity is outlawed? By analogy with the total institutions (such as monasteries) described by Goffman (1961), we can posit the existence of 'total networks' that are organized teleologically, in pursuit of shared goals to the exclusion of other social processes. Such networks require new members to sever all existing social ties to kin and friends in order to pursue mandated goals. Certain terrorist cells and religious cults might require this kind of drastic network pruning as a condition of membership. Such total networks may regard all extraneous affiliations as potential interference with goal accomplishment.

It is possible also to conceive of a network in which serendipity is protected. Any attempt to mobilize resources towards some goal might be regarded as the worst sort of 'interpersonal flatulence' (Burt, 1992: 24–5). Friends meet to socialize. There is no talk of helping the wider network achieve anything. Such talk would meet with incredulity and resistance.

Such a network would permit ties to develop haphazardly as opportunities become available. A network that preserved the possibility of serendipity would tend to be one that experienced some degree of member turnover. Some ties within the network would weaken or disappear over time because of distance or changing interests. Members would enjoy the possibility of chance encounters bringing unexpected benefits in terms of new ideas, resources, and other things that lie outside the normal routine. Without member turnover, new ideas are less likely to enter the network (Carley, 1999).

Goal-directed Networking Exploits Serendipity

Many networks are explicit about appropriating members' personal networks for the purpose of goal achievement. As one practitioner book notes:

> Making contacts and referrals is the *raison-d'être* of a networking club. ... Your new direct contacts willingly give you access to their contacts. They're bridges to your newly expanded second-order zone. ... asking for and giving referrals are requirements. ... A first level referral is a friend of a friend. (Baker, 1994: 265)

This type of network colonizes members' personal lives by asking people to exploit their friendship and kinship contacts to help members sell products, get jobs or otherwise advance the goals of the network.

Serendipitous Networking Undermines Goal-directedness

Practitioner books tend to look askance at networks that have let themselves deteriorate into 'informal and loosely organized ... excuses for having a good time' – clubs that 'meet sporadically, change locations, and impose few rules and regulations' (Baker, 1994: 268). Instead of serious, goal-directed networking activities, some clubs become nothing but 'shmooz-fests that give networking a bad name' (Baker, 1994: 268). The principle of entropy ensures that unless there are active leaders patrolling the boundaries, insisting on rule implementation and managing the process of goal accomplishment, goal-directed network trajectories will lose their teleological dynamic, and network clubs will become a venue for serendipitous encounters.

One Type of Network Process Changes into the Other

Because network trajectories extend over space and time, it is also possible to see alternating or concurrent periods of goal-directedness and serendipity. A network, after achieving its goals, may transform itself into an arena for members to do nothing more than interact. Following goal accomplishment, the relationships among the actors are likely to continue and these relationships may indeed thrive and extend in the absence of any shared goals. For example, members of a job-search network may retain friends from the network after they all find jobs. Goal-directedness may have long ceased to organize interactions but dyads may still socialize because they enjoy each other's company. After a period of change through serendipitous interaction, goal-directedness may once again organize the network into a hierarchical focused unity: the network may discover a new goal.

Goals may be reactivated, therefore, in a network that had ceased to organize itself around goal accomplishment. Goals may also emerge in a network that has grown on serendipitous encounters. For example, a loosely-connected group of friends may form a rotating-credit network for the purpose of helping each other deal with financial needs. The newly-emerged financial goal may come to dominate the interactions of the group, transforming what had been a porous and disorganized interaction process into a highly cohesive set of exchange relationships complete with officeholders and rules of participation.

It is possible to imagine a hybrid process of network development, a trajectory characterized by alternating cycles of goal-directedness and serendipity punctuated by transformation episodes or periods. According to punctuated equilibrium models, transformation periods are times of discontinuous change during which strategies, power, structures and systems are transformed by, and realigned towards, the purposive actions of leading actors (Tushman and Romanelli, 1985). After a period of serendipitous network development, a leader may emerge to orient the network towards goal accomplishment. After another period of time, the newly-focused network may relapse into loose coalitions of actors united by nothing more than the pleasures of sociability. Then, goal-orientation may spring up in another part of the network. Thus, at any particular point in time we may see local centres of goal-orientation together with ties between these centres.

Such complex network dynamics are best modelled by simulation procedures. These have evidenced great promise in unfolding the likely outcomes of different types of starting conditions and assumptions. Research using computational networks (e.g., Carley and Prietula, 1994) and organizational simulations (e.g., Harrison and Carroll, 1991) can provide many useful tests of network theories.

IMPLICATIONS

The typology of network processes contributes to theory in several ways. First, it offers a parsimonious explanation of a wide variety of network trajectories. The contrast between goal-directed teleology and serendipitous muddling-through captures two quite different change processes. The complexities of network change can be analysed as the composite of these primitive processes.

Secondly, our typology provides a foundation for future research. Most of the existing studies on social networks tend to capture snapshots of network processes at one or two periods of time. Without clear network development and change theory, researchers lack guidance concerning how to predict and interpret different network trajectories. Our typology suggests that understanding the underlying assumptions of different network processes is the first step to understanding network change.

The ideas described in our typology are complementary to the insights gained by recent advances in research methodology on longitudinal networks. Our ideas concerning serendipitous processes find echoes in the proposed sequential network model based on stochastic assumptions of actors' tie-sending behaviours over time (Wasserman and Iacobucci, 1986). There is the possibility of using graph theory to study predictions of how a network degenerates into a number of disconnected components (Tutzauer, 1985). Extending structural balance theory to examine reciprocity and transitivity in sociometric choices over time would considerably enhance our understanding of serendipitous tie formation (see Doreian et al., 1996). All of these studies have contributed to better estimation and more refined modelling of dynamic networks with a special focus on micro-structural issues (such as dyadic or triadic patterns). Like much of the existing research, these studies have tended to rely on prior social structures to predict future structures. We anticipate future work in which the presence or absence of initial goal formation processes, together with serendipitous processes of network balance, are important factors in producing network structural change.

As mentioned previously, future work on goal-directed and serendipitous processes in networks can profitably draw upon advances in network simulation. Using binominal distributions and Monte Carlo simulations, researchers can already predict the number of acquaintances in a large network (De Sola Pool and Kochen, 1978). A simulation approach has provided insight into the evolution of group and sub-group structure over time (Zeggelink, 1995). Further, the addition and deletion of nodes and ties in a network over time also lends itself to simulation (Hummon and Fararo, 1995). With a set of process equations and a set of algorithmic statements that govern change, a simulation approach will allow us to model goal-directedness and serendipity in networks under different assumptions.

SUMMARY

By pointing out the implications for individual actors of goal-directed and serendipitous network processes, this chapter contributes to an understanding of the micro–macro links in network formation and change. Individual actors shape the formation and development of social structures through teleological and serendipitous processes; and the trajectories of these social structures offer changing arenas within which actors' own careers are established and promoted. In the next chapter, we offer a summary of the major topics of this book, including an emphasis on the dynamic, fluid nature of social interaction in organizational settings.

RECOMMENDED FURTHER READING

Burt, R.S. and Ronchi, D. 1990. Contested control in a large manufacturing plant. In J. Wessie and H. Flap (eds), *Social networks through time*, pp. 121–57. Utrecht, Netherlands: ISOR.
A brilliant analysis of the change over 30 years in the network of relationships within a factory and how these relationships connected to the communities around the factory. This chapter is both a methodological *tour de force* and a startling depiction of how invisible but powerful social structures can control opportunities.

Gulati, R. and Gargiulo, M. 1999. Where do interorganizational networks come from? American Journal of Sociology, 104: 1439–93.
Innovative study of how interorganizational networks emerge: organizations create stable relationships with trusted partners, and, over time, these ties accumulate into a network that provides the organizations in the network with information about future alliance partners.

Human, S.E. and Provan, K.G. 2000. Legitimacy building in the evolution of small-firm multilateral networks: A comparative study of success and demise. *Administrative Science Quarterly*, 45: 327–65.
A valuable analysis of the development of two small-firm networks over time, showing why one network failed while the other succeeded.

Newcomb, T.M. 1961. *The acquaintance process*. New York: Holt, Rinehart & Winston.
One of the first and best studies of how relationships among strangers (transfer students at the University of Michigan) rapidly coalesce into stable patterns given frequent opportunities for social interaction (within shared living quarters). Relevant data are also conveniently available for analysis as part of the UCINET software package.

6 Towards a Poststructuralist Network Approach to Organizations

In this chapter we both synthesize and extend the developments we have articulated in the previous chapters. Building on the contributions of organizational social network research, we offer a set of ideas that comprise a significant extension of structuralist thinking. In emphasizing the importance of fluidity, subjectivity, textuality and pluralism for network research, we draw upon ideas current in the humanities and in other intellectual traditions rarely accessed by social network researchers. Our intent is to open space for significant departures from the relatively restricted agenda that has characterized social network research.

Much social network research adopts some version of critical realism in attributing to network structure an immutability and solidity that is removed from the sphere of individual action. From a critical-realist perspective, actors 'unavoidably find themselves operating in pre-structured contexts and interests that shape the social struggles in which they are implicated' (Reed, 1997: 31). Structure, according to this view, is the product of 'underlying generative mechanisms' (Reed, 1997: 32) that are removed from the control of individual actors. This ontological orientation of social network research leads to comments concerning the apparent helplessness of individual actors to resist powerful forces over which they have no more control than molecules over the laws of the universe. The holy grail of research from this perspective is the establishment of a 'socio-cognitive quantum mechanics' derived from the discovery of 'simple learning mechanisms operating within a system of constraints' (Carley, 1999: 25).

While we applaud the search for parsimonious explanations of complex phenomena, we base our research model on the establishment of strong theory rather than on the hope that a set of simple rules will explain the complexity of all organizational social network patterns. In outlining the possibilities of theory applicable to social network research (Chapter 3), we hope to have established a pluralist foundation for the different levels and issues that routinely characterize organizational social network research. We seek not to deny structuralist ideas, but to provide theories applicable to organizational contexts in which actors routinely constitute the network constraints within which action proceeds. In exploring the subjective and dispositional sources of network variation (Chapter 4), we have tried to deepen our knowledge of how human action creates and changes network structures. And in our analysis of network dynamics (Chapter 5) we have shown how theory and research considered in the previous chapters can motivate renewed attention to the patterns of network evolution.

There is little doubt that structuralism has given organizational network research a useful focus on the formal properties of organizational systems. As with other structural approaches, social network analysis locates actors in the whole field of interdependent forces instead of isolating actors as units of analysis. The emphasis is on how actors connect to others within and across boundaries, and the antecedents and consequences of such connections. The hope is to do more than merely depict networks of relations. The aspiration of all structural analysis is to discern the deeper organizing principles that are assumed to produce and reproduce the structures that shape action.

Paradoxically, it is this emphasis on underlying forces that tends to restrict the theoretical provenance of network research in organizational settings. As suggested by the structuralist approach, many individual actors (such as small and medium-size organizations) may be constrained by elements in the macro-environment (such as government agencies and large organizations) that pre-exist the smaller actors' entry into organizational fields. However, even these smaller actors are likely to have some discretion concerning the structure of social networks that connect them to their immediate resource providers (see Pfeffer and Salancik, 1978). In this sense, actors help determine the structures of dependence and constraint within which they operate. Structuralist agendas that ignore or neglect individual agency fail, therefore, to articulate how actors constitute and change organizational networks. As one sympathetic critique concluded, network analysis 'fails to show exactly how it is that intentional, creative human action serves in part to constitute those very social networks that so powerfully constrain actors in turn' (Emirbayer and Goodwin, 1994: 1413).

In all of our thinking and research, we build upon the achievements of structuralist research while seeking to avoid the restrictions of the self-declared structuralist paradigm. This structuralist paradigm is certainly pervasive and is sometimes freely acknowledged by those aware of the intellectual roots of network research (e.g., Hummon and Carley, 1993). Thus Berkowitz, in his influential treatment of social network analysis, writes as follows:

> All contemporary approaches to scientific enquiry which refer to themselves as 'structural,' 'structuralist,' or 'structural analytic' share an abiding concern with patterning in events, with relations among elementary components of systems or structures, and with the primacy of systemic transformations in shaping processes. (Berkowitz, 1982: 159)

More recently, Mizruchi (1994), in tracing the roots of network analysis (including organizational network analysis) to the structural sociology of Durkheim, Marx and Simmel (as well as to the French structuralism of Lévi-Strauss), writes: 'The primary tenet of network analysis is that the structure of social relations determines the content of those relations' (Mizruchi, 1994: 330). It is this emphasis on structural determinism that we have challenged.

Thus, we seek to extend selected parts of the structuralist legacy in network analysis while rejecting the notion of a separate paradigm immune from criticism or improvement from other intellectual traditions. To the extent that sociological structuralism gives the network analysis of organizations a theoretical foundation that emphasizes the embeddedness of action in systems of relations, we believe we should extend rather than reject the structuralist legacy. As the chapters in our book have indicated, we see a need to extend structuralist thinking beyond the Durkheimian notion of networks as constraining social facts that pre-empt individual agency; and beyond the idea that the structures of social networks exist as strata removed from the realm of volitional interaction. Social networks are constraints that individuals cooperate to build and maintain. Rather than being static structures, networks represent the dynamic interplay of micro-processes that operate at the level of cognition and interpersonal interaction. Our view represents a version of poststructuralism that enlarges network approaches to organizations to include links to other intellectual traditions (especially those in the humanities). We offer here a fresh look at the contemporary possibilities available to social network research from a poststructuralist perspective.

GOING BEYOND STRUCTURALISM: EXTENDING THE POSSIBILITIES OF NETWORK RESEARCH ON ORGANIZATIONS

Agency

In Table 6.1 we list some of the defining characteristics of our poststructuralist perspective together with implications for organizational social network

TABLE 6.1	
Poststructuralism and social networks	
Characteristics of poststructuralism	**Implications for network research**
Bringing the subject back in as active agent engaged in the structuring of networks through action and perception.	Renewed attention to subjective perceptions of networks, intersubjectivity and agency.
Challenge myth of progress.	Recovery of historically important work.
Emphasis on pluralism, fluidity, subjectivity of structure rather than the solidity of structural forms.	Competing theories; more emphasis on ephemeral relationships, fluidity of identity, heterogeneity.
Society and social science as text.	Language as medium of networks; deconstruction of classics.
Network actors include humans as well as machines, buildings, etc.	Look at connections between human actors and other actors in the environment.

research. At the top of the list is the reintroduction of the active agent into our research agenda. Unlike purely sociological approaches that follow Durkheim in relegating or ignoring the role of the individual in network formation and change (e.g., McPherson et al., 1992), we conceptualize social networks as responsive to the ongoing aspirations and efforts of individual actors. These actors' perceptions of their positions in networks are important determinants of network change (see Burt, 1982). Actors' perceptions and beliefs form inter-subjective cognitive networks that interrelate with and respond to the networks of interaction that are the more familiar focus of research attention. Actors believe that they are competing with others they perceive may replace them in the network; or they cooperate with others whom they believe have network connections that are useful. Perceptions drive actions that change networks. One actor may perceive that another actor is friendly and may feel obliged to reciprocate the friendship, and thus a social tie is born. Actor A may perceive that two other actors A regards as A's friends are disconnected, and therefore feels obliged to bring the two together. Thus the social group is born. These connections proceed irrespective of whether A's perceptions are accurate.

In Chapter 4 we presented an extensive treatment of how individualist approaches to social networks can restore agency to the structuralist paradigm while retaining the distinctive structuralist emphasis on systems of relationships. From a poststructuralist perspective, we can add to the material in that chapter an abiding concern with how agency and subjectivity are themselves constituted in organizations through interpersonal relationships that exert concertive control (e.g., Barker, 1993) and that shape the taken-for-granted roles that delimit the possibilities of action (e.g., Barley, 1990). Thus, post-structuralist network research goes beyond the current paradigm in emphasizing the ways interactions create patchworks of localized structure that maintain the intersubjective interpretations characteristic of small groups. These intersubjective interpretations can be coercive in their effects on the emotional experiences of fragmented groups (e.g., Krackhardt and Kilduff, 1990), but there is always the subversive possibility that, given multiple subjectivities and differing possibilities for identity congruence (e.g., Polzer et al., 2002), identity management will slip out of the control of corporate culture champions. From the poststructuralist perspective, one looks for the emergence of the 'bricoleur' – the identity entrepreneur who takes fragments of roles, ambiguous relationships and shifting coalitions as the familiar and trusted basis for the establishment of self (see Derrida, 1976: 118). Thus, agency from a poststructuralist perspective suggests examining how the web of subjective interpretations of norms, values and behaviours shifts and changes, with coalitions forming and reforming around specific issues and persons (see Murnighan and Brass, 1991).

Fluidity

From our poststructuralist perspective, organizations are networks of relations in permanent states of flux and transformation. Whereas the conventional model of organizations emphasizes the reassuring predictability of organizational activity, with events occurring each day with an inevitability that recalls the repetition of lines 'uttered by a Hamlet on the stage' (March and Simon, 1958: 143), we emphasize the importance of apparently fleeting relations, cognitions and connections. Very much compatible with this approach is Granovetter's (1973) emphasis on weak ties – defined as more fleeting than the strong ties of daily interaction usually studied in organizational network research. The ephemeral world of weak ties is overlooked in organizational research because weak ties exist between people who rarely meet, and whose relationships are carried in memory more than in regular interaction. Recent theorizing has tended to reduce weak-tie theory to a footnote of the structural-hole approach (Burt, 1992). Although it is true that either a strong tie or a weak tie can bridge across a structural hole, it is also true that strong-tie networks are likely to be more stable than weak-tie networks. People have encounters with strangers every day in organizations. Only some of these encounters are repeated. Yet it is precisely from these fleeting encounters that snippets of gossip, unexpected news, different perspectives and revealing social comparisons arise. Weak ties, therefore, have a special significance from a perspective that sees organizations as constantly in flux. Standard network approaches simply leave this flux out of the picture.

In this book we have also tried to alert social network researchers to the extent to which the fluidity of individual identity depends on the availability of social networks. Individuals with multiple, fluid, contradictory identities tend to be those who move between different network configurations. Particular identities become salient as individuals enter and leave social situations in which characteristics are underrepresented. For example, gender becomes a more salient feature of identity for women compared to men in an organization composed mainly of men, whereas ethnicity becomes more salient for those in the minority compared to those belonging to the ethnic majority. People's identifications tend to be influenced by the individual's distinctive characteristics in the social space (Mehra et al., 1998).

Network research has tended to ignore attributes of individuals because of the focus on relations rather than fixed entities. Major theorists have disparaged mainstream sociological research because of its supposed reliance on 'fixed categories of social actors who share similar characteristics: "women," "the elderly," "blue-collar workers," "emerging nations," and so on' (Wellman, 1988a: 15). But this kind of critique represents little more than a crude caricature of sociology. We have built extensively on ideas first articulated by Georg Simmel, regarded by some as 'the first sociologist of post-modernity' (Stauth and Turner, 1988: 16). From a Simmelian perspective, actors' attributes are in dynamic interplay with social contexts. There is no fixed set of characteristics that dominates actor identity across social contexts. Instead, each actor's distinctiveness emerges from the unique pattern of social groups to which the actor belongs (see Kondo, 1990). At the level of individual persons, some of these groups are demographic (gender, ethnicity, religion), some are formal organizations, and some are voluntary associations. Social identity can change as individuals add or subtract organizational memberships, move up or down the hierarchy in terms of holding official positions, or move into or out of social situations in which the distinctiveness of attributes changes. Social network research can help capture the fluidity of identity and thereby go beyond the perpetration of myths concerning the stability of identity categorization.

We are also alert to the ways in which individuals continually constitute the social structures that constrain and enable action. Whereas network research has tended to neglect individual agency in favour of an overemphasis on the ways in which a relatively static social structure determines outcomes (Emirbayer and Goodwin, 1994), we have endeavoured to bring the individual back in (see Kilduff and Krackhardt, 1994) as an active participant in the ongoing perception and creation of structure. As part of this new focus on the active individual, network research from our perspective has focused attention on how self-monitoring personality orientation affects social networks.

Building directly from theory concerning the nature of the self in the social world, research on self-monitoring in organizational settings has shown that the high self-monitoring chameleons (i.e., people who can change their attitudes and behaviours to appeal to different clusters of people) tend to create for themselves central positions in friendship and workflow networks over time (Mehra et al., 2001). In contrast, the true-to-themselves, low self-monitors tend to build and be loyal to clique-like friendship circles (see Snyder, 1987, for a review of self-monitoring research). Using the self-monitoring lens to understand the social dynamics of networks draws attention to paradoxical aspects of the self that have been neglected in the modernist emphasis on stability and consistency. High self-monitors are consistently inconsistent, and it is the constancy of their inconsistency that enables them to influence the structures of their worlds in terms of spanning across social divides. Low self-monitors are consistently cliquish in terms of preferring to build stable clusters of relations that endure over time.

The Object is Subjective

For poststructuralists there is no methodology that allows the researcher an unmediated, objective representation of reality, whether this reality be a physical object or a social network (Rorty, 1979). Poststructuralists accept that different representations of reality can mutually co-exist. From this perspective, such complexity is to be preferred to an insistence that one particular representation of a social network be privileged over another as the 'true' network.

Most previous research treats social networks as social facts in the Durkheimian sense of external, objective constraints that determine the outcomes of individual actors. Note, for example, this definition of a social network in one of the founding texts of the field: 'a regular, persistent pattern in the behavior of the elementary parts of a social system' (Berkowitz, 1982: 1). Network research tends to proceed from a naive ontology that takes as unproblematic the objective existence and persistence of patterns, elementary parts and social systems. The emphasis is placed on 'concrete relations between individuals' (Degenne and Forse, 1999: 2). Even where utility perceptions are introduced into discussions of social networks (e.g., Burt, 1982), the existence of objective so-called 'concrete' networks of social relations are never questioned. As David Krackhardt has pointed out with respect to theories that try to incorporate perceptions of so-called objective networks: 'The assumption that an actor's perceptions of similarity to others is a direct and derivable function of any kind of "objective" similarity to others is tenuous' (Krackhardt, 1987: 112).

A poststructuralist perspective challenges the taken-for-granted stability and objectivity of social networks with a reminder of the fragility and subjectivity of network relations. Concurrent with the rise of poststructuralist thinking has been an increasing interest in the ways in which social networks exist as cognitive social structures. The leading researcher in this area has gone so far as to suggest: 'One should not bother collecting behavioral data, since they do such a poor job of capturing the cognitions which live in people's heads' (Krackhardt, 1987: 110). Research on cognitive social structures has revealed that individuals have widely differing cognitions of the social relations of themselves and others (Krackhardt, 1990; Kumbasar et al., 1994); that cognitions of those close to and far from the individual tend to be driven by a balance theory logic (Krackhardt and Kilduff, 1999); that 'true' social structures can be constructed in several different ways by researchers depending on assumptions about data (Krackhardt, 1987); and that cognitions about social ties can be more predictive of important outcomes in organizational settings than conventionally measured ties (Kilduff and Krackhardt, 1994).

In short, so-called 'concrete' social relations tend to be constructs in the minds of researchers rather than objective patterns in the lives of individuals. Aggregating individual perceptions of social ties can help create pictures of networks, but these pictures will differ depending on the methodological assumptions of the researcher.

Nothing Outside the Text?

Derrida's (1976: 158) famous dictum ('There is nothing outside the text') reminds us of the extent to which social science in general has become a text-driven endeavour: researchers write, not just in relation to the events and structures in the lives of their subjects, but in relation to other texts (Latour, 1987). Some of our most important research in the organizational arena occupies itself exclusively with texts about organizations rather than about organizations themselves (e.g., Barley et al., 1988; Mizruchi and Fein, 1999). It is important, therefore, to consider research as a form of writing, not as a mirror that reflects an undistorted view of reality.

The extent to which apparently objective research reports are constituted as rhetorical projects is the concern of analytical procedures summarized under the rubric of deconstruction. The deconstructive approach assumes that all writing, whether it be theoretical, methodological or statistical, is inherently literary. There is no such thing as a neutral style, a mere stating of the facts. Deconstruction directs attention, in network research, to the extent to which the ways in which the article is written determines the truth claims that it makes.

Deconstruction is particularly sceptical *vis-à-vis* textual claims concerning special access to truth, to matters too evident to be even worth discussing, to conclusions that are missing their premises, or to inferences that should have been made, given a set of assumptions, but that are missing. Deconstruction asks questions that are rarely formulated from modernist perspectives, such as: Which data are absent from the text and why? And why is one member of a pair of binary terms (such as structural equivalence/cohesion) subordinated to the other in this text?

One of the most powerful deconstructive gestures is to reveal to the reader a hidden text, present for all to see once its absence is made present by an analysis that brings it to the attention of the reader. One example was a deconstruction of March and Simon's foundational book *Organizations* (1958) showing that the text replicated the moves of predecessors it condemned, and asserted an ideology or programming that justified the inevitable fractionation of work (Kilduff, 1993). Deconstruction can be a creative process that enriches our understanding of texts rather than impoverishing them.

How could deconstruction be used in social network research? One possible example concerns the recent series of medical diffusion texts that discuss the competing claims of two theoretical explanations for the adoption of new technology by physicians. Whereas one explanation (structural equivalence) emphasizes competition between rivals similarly situated in the social network, the other explanation (cohesion) emphasizes processes of empathic communication and friendship (Burt, 1987: 1289). A careful review of the series of re-analyses shows that all four (Burt, 1987; Marsden and Podolny, 1990; Strang and Tuma, 1993; Van den Bulte and Lilien, 2001) appeared to be analysing the same data included in the original text, but all four omitted from consideration the friendship network data that formed such an important part of the original story of social integration articulated in the classic text by Coleman, Katz and Menzel (1966). The unexplained dropping of the friendship data, replicated in each of the re-analyses, constitutes, according to a deconstruction of these texts, a substantive change to the evidential base on which the inferences of the researchers depend (Kilduff and Oh, 2002). Further, the dropping of the friendship data forms part of a consistent narrative in a re-analysis that extols not social integration but rivalry and competition.

Deconstruction draws attention to the ways in which the narrative structure of the text forms an overarching schema that guides every aspect of the writing. Social scientific texts tell stories about the world, and in order to evaluate such texts it is important to focus on this storytelling. Deconstruction focuses not just on what is absent from the text (e.g., analysis of the friendship network), but also on what is made present. In the first two of the re-analyses of the medical diffusion data (Burt, 1987; Marsden and Podolny, 1990), data were 'imputed' in order to bring into the analysis specialist physicians excluded by the original researchers. Deconstruction alerts the reader to the fictionalization of data in the context of a research document that purports to be a reflection of the world. Thus, a deconstruction of the re-analyses of the medical diffusion data exposes both what is absent (the friendship network) and what has been made present (imputed data on specialists' adoption behaviours).

To a remarkable degree, the re-analyses of the medical diffusion data illustrate the extent to which network research has become a textual endeavour. The medical diffusion data were treated in the re-analyses as a stand-alone text, readily available for creative reinterpretation, without the necessity for any reference to influences from outside the text. As a literary critic might predict, there is no end to the interpretation of free-floating signifiers. The chain of texts offering stories about how physicians in small-town America in 1953–54 wrote prescriptions for the antibiotic tetracycline is by no means at an end.

What is striking about this chain of interlinked texts is that each new article used as its point of reference the previous text rather than the actual community of physicians. Even the original authors never visited the physicians. Further, results have directly contradicted each other not because of any differences in the supposed reality of the social networks or the behaviour of the physicians, but because of the differing interpretative lenses of the researchers. And finally, so text-bound have the research endeavours been that each researcher has meticulously repeated the arbitrary decisions of the previous researchers with respect, for example, to something as major as ignoring the influence of the friendship network on patterns of drug adoption.

In the series of texts dealing with the diffusion of medical innovation, grand narratives may have influenced choices concerning judgement calls. A view of the world as consisting of actors seeking personal advantage is one of the dominant narratives in the social sciences, harking back at least to the work of Adam Smith. In social network research, this narrative depicts individual actors maximizing advantage through the strategic development of network links. Applied to the medical diffusion data set, this narrative naturally leads to the assumption that physicians in small-town USA in the early 1950s were using network links in the competition for patients. Thus, small variations in patterns of actors' social relations were exaggerated to maximize differences between otherwise relatively identically-positioned actors (Burt, 1987). If actors' relations with others were weighted strictly in accordance with distance (so that close ties were weighted proportionately more than distant ties), 'every physician is to some degree equivalent to every other physician in his or her city' (Marsden and Podolny, 1990: 212), and there is no support for the competition-between-structurally-equivalent-alters narrative.

Deconstruction is now so familiar that it has even lent its name to one of the Strategic Management Society's annual meetings! The hope is that by questioning the taken-for-granted meanings of a text, and by showing the operation of hidden and even subversive texts, researchers can deconstruct the often esoteric methodological claims of network research, encouraging more transparency. This is difficult work, however. The popularity of the term 'deconstruction' has not been matched by the arduous process of deconstructive criticism in network and management studies.

Poststructuralism, therefore, focuses on the process by which social reality is constructed through writing, a writing that derives in many cases from taken-for-granted grand narratives. Poststructuralist writers take exception to the deployment of grand theorizing that imposes frameworks on data without concern for the context in which the data were collected. The critique of meta-narratives (such as Marxism and structuralism) is part of an overall scepticism towards dogmatic agendas (see Lyotard, 1984). In the social sciences, we often hear calls by those wedded to positivist research for a radical simplification of theory (e.g., Pfeffer, 1993) and for an embrace of scientific canons of parsimony and falsifiability (e.g., Berkowitz, 1982). Poststructuralists distrust those who seek to sweep away alternative research paradigms, who derogate whole areas of research (such as social psychology) as consisting of, in the words of one structuralist writer, 'non-answers to ... non-questions' (Mayhew, 1980: 365).

Pluralism

In rejecting systems of overarching propositions, poststructuralists emphasize the multivocal and equivocal nature of the world in which we live. Research is needed that registers the differences and heterogeneity of this world as well as the surprising commonalities that link people across traditional boundaries. Rather than capturing exclusively the stable patterns of ties in bureaucratic organizations, poststructuralist network research aims to capture also the ephemeral, fleeting aspects of social ties. A poststructuralist social network agenda would necessarily require much more detailed attention to social contexts in which ties emerge and change. We would expect to see more careful case studies of network ties and less cavalier neglect of the embeddedness of social ties in particular local sites.

Social network research has tended to be driven by methods, especially those conveniently packaged in network software programs. But there is no reason why insight into social networks cannot proceed on the basis of case studies (e.g., Burt and Ronchi, 1990; Larson, 1992), participant observation (Kapferer, 1972), or even novels (e.g., the work of Proust on how social mobility is facilitated by social capital). Poststructuralism adds to this eclecticism an emphasis on language and texts, an emphasis not restricted just to textual analysis of research reports (Clifford and Marcus, 1986), but also including analyses of how textual elements in society interrelate to affect outcomes (Dorst, 1989).

From a poststructuralist perspective, society itself can be read and analysed as a text (Taborsky, 1997). Social networks between people in society are part of the constantly inscribed and reinscribed meanings that people create every day as they reaffirm identities. In this ongoing process of network construction and creation, language (both spoken and written) takes on a ritualistic, repetitive character well captured by the Japanese term '*aisatsu*': ceremonial greetings that allow people the opportunity to forge connections across the boundaries of privacy and strangeness. (See Abell, 1987, for one example of how narrative structures can be analysed as networks; and Van Maanen 1988 and 1995, for analyses of writing style as theory.)

One poststructuralist approach almost neglected by network researchers is the actor-network perspective that examines how human and non-human networks engage (Latour, 1987). The exclusive focus on human interaction in standard social network analysis ignores the powerful relationships people form with machines, texts, animals and buildings. In organizations, for example, people establish relationships with their computers, relationships that involve anger, affection, talk, collaboration, caring and criticism. People even come to think of themselves in terms of the technology they interact with (Turkle, 1984). Such intense identifications with technology can change network patterns in organizations.

Although we proclaim our adherence to a plurality of approaches to social networks in organizations, we recognize that evaluating such diverse research poses significant challenges. From a poststructuralist perspective, the criterion for the evaluation of social network research must be excellence rather than adherence to the tenets of any particular paradigm. Excellence itself is assessed not through compatibility with preconceived notions of parsimony and predictive validity, but by the consensus of the community of research practice (Fish, 1980). One of the aims of this book is to enlarge the community of research practice in the social network arena so that innovative work is encouraged rather than excluded. Work that states the obvious (however rigorous its methods, however objective its prose) not only fails to contribute to social science, it runs the risk of bringing the whole enterprise of social science into disrepute.

Poststructuralist research tends towards small-scale, individual efforts rather than large-scale research teams (see Weick, 1983). From a poststructuralist perspective, dominant grand narratives are to be avoided, and fragmentation of voices is likely to lead to a pleasing heterogeneity. Thus poststructuralism is incompatible with the idea of paradigm incommensurability that some in the social network field endorse. Calls for devotion to paradigmatic unity are perilous because they reduce the ability to combine diverse approaches and remove social network research from the concerns of a wide variety of stakeholders. Efforts to exclude from social network analysis consideration of complex constructs such as 'symbols, meanings, and values' (Wellman and Berkowitz, 1988: 5) in favour of the analysis of pure structure are resisted by poststructural social network researchers, as are attempts to specify restricted menus of authorized methods.

The Truth is in the Question

One of the major differences between any version of poststructuralist network research and any version of structuralist network research concerns the approach to truth. Structuralists seek universal laws of social behaviour, whereas poststructuralists accept that the aim of social science is not generalizability as the be-all and end-all of social theory (see Giddens, 1984: xix), but discovery. To pursue universal laws of social networks is to risk repeated failure, given that multiple contingencies affect networks, including local conditions and the familiarity of actors with the so-called generalizations that the researchers are attempting to substantiate. We sometimes forget that interest in social networks in the media is high and that many educated people are now familiar with basic network concepts such as centrality and structural holes through the work of such first-class popularizers as Baker (1994, 2000) and Gladwell (2000). So-called laws of behaviour can be flouted or exploited by people who have been taught how they operate, much as one can successfully overcome cognitive dissonance in decision-making once one recognizes its familiar symptoms. Attempting to impose unchangeable laws on the thoughts and social behaviours of changeable humans is tantamount to bidding the ocean to stop invading the beach.

A poststructuralist social network approach would seek not to uncover eternal truths, but to open new questions for exploration. Rather than seeking to nail down every last aspect of some paradigmatic set of network laws, post-structuralist research would pursue enquiries into previously unexplored domains of social networking in organizational contexts. Poststructuralists recognize that researchers produce highly personal texts that permit both self-fulfilment and the creation of interpretative communities (see Latour, 1987). Poststructuralism encourages cross-fertilization across research domains in the pursuit of distinctive contributions to understanding.

An important and sometimes overlooked aspect of poststructural enquiry is the provision of public benefit from research. Poststructuralist research tends to be located in actual organizations, not simulated ones, it incorporates a focus on those trapped inside failing institutions such as school children in inner cities, and it tends to draw attention to those on the margins (e.g., Mehra et al., 1998) and those who cross taken-for-granted organizational boundaries (e.g., Cassell, 1996). Just as teachers can transform classrooms through the use of innovative pedagogy (see Giroux, 1992), so network researchers can strive to improve the world of organizations by doing research relevant to practice, and by reminding people, including the research community, of the practical implications of their research (see Hambrick, 1994; Kilduff and Kelemen, 2001).

Distinctiveness

A drastic difference between standard network practice and an emerging post-structuralist social network approach is the move away from a complete reliance on survey research and other methods that tend to homogenize the variations in organizations. The poststructuralist researcher is likely to be interested not just in generalities but also in distinctiveness, both at the individual level and at the organizational level. The specific patterns of networks in an organization are likely to be of interest. In this sense, a poststructuralist network approach harks back to the anthropological roots of the field. Urban anthropologists, such as the Hawthorne researchers (Roethlisberger and Dickson, 1939), were similar to other field anthropologists (e.g., Kapferer, 1972) in taking infinite care to describe the details of connections in work groups. The Hawthorne researchers described six networks of interaction between the

14 members of the bank wiring room, and went into considerable detail concerning psychology and motivation. Poststructuralist enquiry refuses to throw aside past social science in the pursuit of a mythical progress towards better and better research practice. From a poststructuralist perspective, excellent social science from whatever era is part of the accessible canon that all of us can draw upon. Poststructuralism debunks the myth that current social science is inevitably superior to that of the past.

For poststructuralists, the purpose of research has nothing to do with the celebration of statistical significance and everything to do with the discovery of meaning. How is it that people in organizations create networks that then constrain them? Can small changes in local network structure affect the overall network patterning, and if so, how? What networking patterns are likely to restrict people in organizational settings from accomplishing apparently attainable goals? Do the stories that individuals tell about themselves and others form narrative networks that channel meaning and identity throughout the organization? These are a few of the issues that poststructuralist research might pursue: local themes anchored in specific times and places that speak to our deep-seated curiosity concerning patterns of interaction.

CONCLUSION

As applied to the field of organizational social networks, poststructuralist critiques barely register as yet, because there has been little work that explicitly follows a poststructuralist approach (but see Breiger, 2002). On the contrary, social network research often identifies itself as within the structuralist tradition, different from the continental structuralism of Lévi-Strauss, Althusser and Lacan, but certainly affiliated with overall structuralist emphases on relations expressed in matrix algebra, and on research that neglects cultural and historical context in favour of underlying patterns (see Degenne and Forse, 1999: 93–5). Standard structuralist analyses of how chains of terms are substituted for each other over time (e.g., Lacan, 1968) clearly relate to the social network emphasis on the chaining of vacancies in job markets (e.g., White, 1970). Similarly, structuralist emphases on binary relations (e.g., Lévi-Strauss, 1963) are mirrored in the social network penchant for signalling the presence and absence of relations with zeros and ones. The social network modern breakthrough conception of structural equivalence finds clear parallels in structuralist emphases on the equivalence of elements in ordinary language, elements that can, like structurally equivalent alters, be substituted for each other without disturbing the system of which they are a part (De Saussure, 1939).

Thus, the social network approach is susceptible to the poststructuralist critique that has successfully challenged the assumptions of other structuralist traditions. What might a poststructuralist social network approach look like? There would be much greater attention to the culture and history of social contexts. Claims for the universal truth of any set of principles (such as structural equivalence), or the reduction of complex patterns to simple ones, would be subject to sceptical enquiry. The attributes of the actor, almost wholly neglected within the social network approach, would be reintroduced to supplement the reliance on matrices of binary connections, but greater attention would also be focused on the social construction of actors, agency and subjectivity. The search for the one true underlying structure would give way to a recognition of the possibility of multiple 'true' structures, and an acceptance of the importance of subjective perceptions. Classical texts would be re-examined critically and constructively for neglected insights and unstated assumptions. Bridges would be built between the mathematics of social network analysis and the poetics of the humanities. The grip of overarching theory would be loosened sufficiently to permit neglected topics to be pursued. A set of social network approaches concerned with text and language in organizational settings would spring up, possibly tied to issues of fluidity and identity. And the full panoply of modernist methods and algorithms, so painstakingly invented by a generation of researchers, would be used and enhanced as social network analysis changed itself in a poststructuralist direction.

Instead of achieving the utopia of its own formidable paradigm complete with theories, methods and software, an organizational social network approach influenced by poststructuralism would resemble a loosely-connected archipelago, with many links to neighbouring disciplines in the social sciences and humanities. Such research would still have its distinctive emphasis on relations, on network diagrams and sociograms, on inventive algorithms and on bridging the micro–macro divide. But research articles would tend to be less abstract and more tied to the organizational context, less removed from daily affairs and more self-consciously historical and cultural, less ready to impose the straitjacket of theory on resisting data and more open to exploration. In short, social network research would tend to be filled with the life of organizations rather than resting content with the abstractions of structure.

Does poststructuralism itself run the risk of turning into a dominant metanarrative that controls the research agenda for social science? There is a sense in which much of the poststructuralist agenda is becoming acceptable practice in many areas of social science. Outside the social network arena we certainly see more scepticism towards grand theory and a growing preference for small-scale ethnographic research on a menu of topics that include fluidity of identity, hegemony and marginalization. The danger of poststructuralism becoming a dominant paradigm is considerably lessened by the pluralism and fragmentation that this approach values. There is no interest from a poststructuralist perspective in establishing a new hegemony to replace the old. Rather, poststructuralist topics and approaches are likely to enliven and complicate the field of social network research as the structural paradigm connects to new thinking in the humanities and across the academy.

SUMMARY

This chapter presents some selected ideas from a poststructuralist perspective in order to connect social network research to intellectual currents in the humanities and other areas of social science. This bridging of structural holes offers many possibilities for renewed research emphases on a range of topics. The poststructuralist incredulity towards metanarrative implies a critical examination of the structuralist underpinnings of social network research. Structure as a stable, objective and concrete set of relations gives way to an emphasis on the fluidity, subjectivity and ephemerality of social networks. Diverse research topics are added to the social network agenda, with special emphasis on players at the margins and neglected voices. The structuralist dream of establishing a set of network laws becomes less important than the exploration of the wide range of network processes and outcomes evident over time and in different organizational settings. Prior work, such as the classics in the field, are rehabilitated and critically examined for insights, with all excellent work regarded as simultaneously available to the research community. Organizational language of all kinds is regarded as the medium of network relations, with organizations examined as textual productions, full of rhetorical claims constituted and disseminated by social networks.

RECOMMENDED FURTHER READING

Breiger, R.L. 2002. Poststructuralism in organizational studies. *Research in the Sociology of Organizations*, 19: 295–305.
In this review of research that overcomes the 'self-imposed isolation' of structural approaches, Breiger discusses the 'getting and manipulation of identities through social networks' and the ways in which network theory is moving closer to perspectives of action, discourse and symbolic representation.

Emirbayer, M. and Goodwin, J. 1994. Network analysis, culture, and the problem of agency. *American Journal of Sociology*, 99: 1411–54.
A lucid critique of the social network approach that complements what we have to say in this chapter.

Kilduff, M. and Mehra, A. 1997. Postmodernism and organizational research. *Academy of Management Review*, 22: 453–81.
A review of the implications of poststructuralist and postmodern ideas for research on organizations.

7 Conclusion

The social network approach to organizations consists of a distinctive set of concepts that focus on systems of relations that can be represented and analysed graphically and quantitatively. Major issues facing social network research in organizational contexts include how actors constitute the ties that cluster together into groups, whether actors recognize the constraints and opportunities that their network positions imply, and the consequences that flow not just from network positions and roles, but also from changes to such positions and roles.

The range of methods and algorithms devoted to network issues bewilders even the sophisticated, and without strong theory to guide the use of methods few research discoveries are likely to be made. In examining the embeddedness of actors in social networks, their social capital accumulations and the extent to which they bridge across structural divides, guiding theory is critical for the identification of antecedents and consequences. When is embeddedness an anchor that restricts mobility and when is it a platform from which initiatives are launched? What are the uses and abuses of social capital, the costs and benefits of social ties? Is bridging a structural hole always the recommended solution to the organizational actor's dilemma? In trying to answer such questions, theory-driven analyses are not just recommended, they are required if we are to have any hope of going beyond the mere accumulation of data sets.

We elaborated three categories of theory that can guide the use of network methods of enquiry: imported, home-grown and exported theory. In the imported category, mathematical graph theory, despite its profusion of practical uses in the depiction of networks and in the provision of useful terms, has yet to yield a commensurate theoretical harvest in organizational settings. Yet we think it can help us unlock some of the implications of structural configurations in organizations, building on the innovative work we reviewed. Social psychology provides the richest borrowed set of perspectives for theory discovery relevant to network issues. This is not surprising given the long history of mutual influence between network researchers and social psychologists, with both groups drawing continuing inspiration and ideas from such pioneers as Lewin, Heider, Homans, Festinger and others. In this book, we draw specific attention to two approaches that go beyond conventional treatments of the social psychology of networks and that offer considerable potential for future work: cognitive network theory and an emergent theory of how personality affects social structure. Far from separating the network paradigm from the live currents in the rest of the social sciences, we recommend drawing energy from these currents in order to enliven the possibilities of network analysis. We also see continued export of network ideas into various organizational theories, resulting in distinctively hybrid approaches.

In terms of the dynamic analysis of organizational social networks, we avoided the temptation of writing a chapter of complaint concerning the predilection of researchers to focus on static treatments of networks. Instead, we offered an original approach to network formation and development. As ideal types, goal-directed and serendipitous processes are quite distinct in their operation and in the trajectories they produce. We look forward to more work concerning how these fundamental processes unfold in organizational settings.

In accessing ideas from the poststructuralist repertoire relevant to network research, we run the risk of inflaming those who have sought to maintain the purity of the social network paradigm. But we view with concern efforts to isolate network research from countervailing intellectual traditions. The robust set of concepts, methods, ideas and theories that comprise network approaches can only benefit from engagement with the intellectual ferment in neighbouring disciplines. Rather than defend structuralist assumptions against all-comers, we prefer to enliven and enrich our research endeavours through engagement with concepts of fluidity, pluralism, subjectivity and textuality. The appeal of network research has always been its sheer eclecticism – its reach across disciplines as diverse as anthropology, psychology, sociology, mathematics and management. From the path-breaking work of the Hawthorne researchers to the poststructuralist writings of Ronald Breiger (2002), network research at its best stretches across structural holes and connects remote intellectual traditions.

FUTURE RESEARCH DIRECTIONS

We do not aim in this book to provide a comprehensive review of current work – such reviews are available elsewhere (see, for example, the chapters in Baum, 2002; and Flap et al., 1998). Our interest is to provoke new research and thinking concerning organizational social networks. We have promoted a view of network research as eclectic rather than purist, as directed towards substantively important topics rather than as consumed with methodological niceties, and as intellectually engaged with other scholarly traditions rather than as an isolated paradigm. Where will this enhanced view of network research take us in the years ahead? We foresee several major trends in network research.

First, we expect to see a burgeoning of theory-building and data analysis concerning network forms of organizing within and between organizations. The issues we discussed in the previous chapter are likely to loom large in this research endeavour. We are likely to see increased research emphasizing the fluidity of organizing arrangements compared to the stability of the Weberian lens through which researchers have conventionally viewed organizations. The issue of whether 'networking' can be considered a new system logic for organizations is likely to receive continued attention (e.g., DiMaggio, 2001). As part of this attention, the focus is likely to include more work on network change. Whereas research on inter-firm connections has relied on relatively stable ties such as interlocking directorates, relatively fleeting ties between partners may be the focus of future work. In rapidly moving environments the key resource is knowledge innovation, and this resource tends to emerge in the interstices between organizational boundaries (Powell et al., 1996). Similarly, within organizations, the emphasis on the relatively stable world of workflow, advice and friendship networks is likely to expand to include questions of how such stability is maintained, under what circumstances it is challenged, and the implications of such challenges to stability for organizational learning (e.g., Barley, 1990).

The old paradigm of research took the network as an objective fixed entity that could be considered a 'social fact'. New research is likely to proceed on very different epistemological grounds. Cognitions about networks are likely to receive increased research attention as people try to understand the ways in which the relatively invisible bonds that bind individual actors together in the absence of legal contracts operate. Why are some ties regarded as trustworthy by some actors but not by others? Are there predictable biases in the perceptions of network ties on the part of those involved in such ties, and on the part of observers? Do perceptions facilitate the provision of resources through network conduits? These kinds of questions have yet to be answered, but could inform us concerning the trust-based governance systems that substitute for formal legal ties in and between organizations.

We are likely to see a paradoxical double movement of research interest – both towards including individual attributes as important determinants of network properties and towards investigating quite different relational units, such as texts. There is no doubt that the individual is back in network analysis despite the efforts of some structuralists to reduce the individual to an epiphenomenal residue of network processes. Research on the extent to which individuals have agency in the production and transformation of organizational networks is likely to produce some key discoveries concerning the constraints and opportunities inherent in network emergence and change. We will begin to identify the different types of network associated with different types of people. Building on this enhanced picture of individual agency, network researchers are likely to be empowered to consider the ways in which elements of the human environment, such as texts and machinery, interrelate with each other and with humans. People have relationships with objects in their environments, such as their computers, that are sometimes 'stronger' (i.e., more frequent and longer-lasting) than with many co-workers. But we have tended to leave out these important interactions in charting networks in the workplace. We expect to see more socio-technical approaches to the intersection of human and non-human networks following from discussions of how information itself is a profoundly socially-embedded product (Brown and Duguid, 2000).

In order to reveal the subtleties of such structural interactions, we expect to see more ethnographic studies of network formation and change, and a move away from an exclusive reliance on arm's length analysis of abstracted patterns of relations. Researchers have pointed to the multiple meanings of even the simplest triadic structure as evidence of the need for greater attention to the context within which relationships unfold. Ego may receive advice from A and send advice to B but, without detailed knowledge of the context, we may be unable to decipher which of at least five possible roles (liaison, representative, gatekeeper, itinerant broker, coordinator) ego is playing (Fernandez and Gould, 1994). Although some network researchers continue to call for a 'socio-cognitive quantum mechanics' of human behaviour (Carley, 1999: 25), future research is more likely to emphasize the multiple contingencies and fascinating exceptions that characterize the complex interweavings of social networks in organizational contexts. We are likely to see a burgeoning of research on how network entrepreneurs build and use social capital, on how individuals strive to borrow others' social capital for their own advancement, on how insiders and outsiders differ in their networking strategies, and on the differential benefits of belonging to relatively closed versus relatively diverse social circles. As Burt (2000: 410) writes in his excellent review of these topics, we need more detailed studies of the 'specific network mechanisms responsible for social capital'.

We also expect more research on the dark side of social capital – on the ways in which social network structures distort the opportunities available to qualified actors. Already we know that having contacts in the right places can facilitate job search (Granovetter, 1974) and salary negotiation (Seidel et al., 2000). These help the fortunate but penalize others who, perhaps naively, play by the rules endemic to meritocratic societies. We should be careful not to institutionalize a view of the world as one in which your prestigious contacts override other considerations, or to appear to endorse the view that it is desirable that your inside information helps you (at the expense of others) to 'discover that the price of your stocks will plummet tomorrow' (example used by Burt, 1992: 14). Increased attention to the potential liabilities of social networks (such as the promotion of illegal activity – see Baker and Faulkner, 1993) may help present a more realistic picture of how social networks function in organizational settings (see also Brass and Labianca, 1999).

According to the social network perspective we have elaborated in this book, the complexity of organizational systems inheres not in rationally-planned structures but in fluid participations and understandings between actors. Identities are preserved within well-understood boundaries around elements that appear and disappear over time as self-determining actors connect around tasks and within contexts that are rich with meaning. Research that captures the often-fleeting networks of meaning creation is likely to draw upon a variety of intellectual traditions. Thus, we offer this book in the hope that it will inspire cross-disciplinary work and more enriching conversations between everyone interested in the social world, and in the practice of research. In our view, the study of social networks in and between organizations encompasses just about everything that is of interest concerning human behaviour in such settings. Human beings are by their very nature gregarious creatures, for whom relationships are defining elements of their identities and creativeness. The study of such relationships is therefore the study of human nature itself.

Glossary of Technical Terms

Actor: discrete individual, organization, event or collective social entity that links to others in a network. Also known as 'node'.

Adjacency matrix: a square matrix, usually consisting of zeros and ones, that indicates for each pair of actors in the network whether they are connected or not (i.e., whether they are 'adjacent' to each other or not in the network). Also known as 'sociomatrix' or 'relational matrix'.

Asymmetric tie: one-way tie from A to B, e.g., A gives advice to B, but B doesn't advise A.

Balance: incorporates the notions of reciprocity and transitivity. A network with a high degree of balance is one in which (a) a tie between two people tends to be reciprocated, and (b) if two people have a common tie to a third person, then the two people tend to have a direct tie to each other (i.e., the three actors form a transitive triad).

Betweenness centrality of an actor: the extent to which an actor serves as a potential 'go-between' for other pairs of actors in the network by occupying an intermediary position on the shortest paths connecting other actors.

Block: a subset of a relational matrix, containing actors who have the same or similar relations to other actors and who can be said, therefore, to occupy more or less the same structural position in the network.

Blockmodelling: a technique for partitioning actors into discrete subsets and identifying relationships among the subsets.

Centrality of an actor: the extent to which an actor occupies a central position in the network in one of the following ways: having many ties to other actors (degree centrality), being able to reach many other actors (closeness centrality), connecting other actors who have no direct connections (betweenness centrality), or having connections to centrally located actors (eigenvector centrality).

Centralization of a network: the extent to which a network is centralized around one or a few central actors (Freeman, 1979).

Clique: a group in which (a) all actors have direct ties with all other actors in the group, and (b) there is no outside-the-group actor to whom all group members have a tie.

Closeness centrality of an actor: the extent to which the most direct paths connecting an actor to each of the other actors in a network are short rather than long. This measure is only meaningful for a fully-connected network in which there are no isolated actors. A high closeness score means an actor can access many other actors and is therefore relatively independent of the control of others (see Powell et al., 1996, for an example).

Cognitive map: a representation of an individual's perceptions of who connects to whom in a social system.

CONCOR (convergence of iterated correlations): a procedure that iteratively correlates the rows (or columns) of a matrix until all the entries in the matrix are either +1 or −1. The matrix can then be divided into two blocks with all the relations within blocks having the value of +1, whereas the relations between blocks have the value of −1 (see Wasserman and Faust, 1994: 376–81). The procedure can continue splitting each block into two blocks of equivalent actors at the discretion of the analyst.

Connectedness: a connected network is one in which every actor can reach every other actor either directly or through an intermediary: there are no isolates. One can also measure relative connectedness as the ratio of pairs of actors that are mutually reachable divided by the total number of pairs of actors in the network (Krackhardt, 1994: 95–6).

Correspondence analysis: a statistical technique that enables the visual portrayal of similarities between two types of entity in the same two-dimensional space. For example, Supreme Court justices and legal issues that come before the Court can be depicted to show, for any justice, the relative closeness of the justice's voting record to the majority with respect to an issue such as 'crime' (Breiger, 2000).

Cutpoint: an actor whose removal from the network results in subsets of actors between whom there is no connection.

Degree centrality: the number of connections that an actor has in a network. It can be broken down into two components: indegree centrality (e.g., the number of people who ask the actor for advice) and outdegree centrality (e.g., the number of people the actor gives advice to).

Density: the number of ties in the network divided by the maximum number of ties that are possible. If all actors are isolates, density = 0, if all actors are connected to all other actors, density = 1.

Dyad: two actors connected by a tie. Thus, we can talk about a friendship dyad consisting of two friends.

Egocentric network: the social network around ego, including ego's direct ties and the ties among ego's direct ties. Thus Jane's egocentric friendship network would include Jane's connections to her friends and the connections among Jane's friends.

Eigenvector centrality: a measure of actor centrality that takes into account the centrality of the actors to whom the focal actor is connected. Thus, an actor whose three friends have many connections will have higher eigenvector centrality than an actor whose three friends have few connections (Bonacich, 1987).

Embeddedness: generally refers to either the overlap between social ties and economic ties, or the nesting of social ties within other social ties. For example, actors' behaviours are embedded to the extent that they tend to transact with exchange partners who are personal friends or kin; or if their exchange partners tend to transact with each other (Granovetter, 1985; Uzzi, 1996). Actors are also embedded to the extent that all or most of their social ties are within a community that has few ties outside of the community.

Gatekeeper: an actor who transmits information and other resources to the social network from links outside the social network.

Graph theory: a branch of mathematics concerned with nodes, and lines between nodes, that offers a formal basis for network analysis. (See Wasserman and Faust, 1994: Chapter 4, for an introduction.)

Homophily: the tendency for actors to interact with, and share the opinions and behaviours of, other actors similar to themselves on such dimensions as ethnicity, age, educational attainment, gender, etc. (see McPherson et al., 2001, for a review).

Incidence matrix: a two-dimensional display that shows for each actor the 'incidents' in which the actor is involved. For example, an incidence matrix could display whether 20 organizations (the actors) donated or not to 32 civic charities (the incidents). These data could be used to produce two square adjacency matrices: one showing the similarity of each pair of organizations with respect to the range of charities donated to, and the other showing the similarity of each pair of charities with respect to the range of organizations contributing.

Isolate: an actor with no ties to any other actor in the network.

K-plex: a clique-like group containing n actors in which each actor connects to no fewer than $n-k$ other actors in the group. Thus, if $k = 2$ and there are 4 people in the group, each person is connected to at least two other persons in the group.

Multiplexity: the extent to which two actors are connected by more than one type of tie. For example, a pair of actors who are friends and members of the same department have a multiplex tie of value '2'.

N-clique: a clique-like group of actors who can all reach each other through a maximum of n links. Thus in a 2-clique each actor can reach every other actor either through a direct connection or through one intermediary.

Reachability: one actor can reach another actor in the network if there is a path connecting the two actors, that is, a way for actor A to get a message or a resource to actor B either directly or through intermediaries. A reachability matrix is one that represents, for each pair of actors, whether one can reach the other or not. The reachability of a network is the relative ease with which actors can reach each other. Network reachability can be measured as the average number of people reached per person in the network for a one-step process (from A to friends of A), a two-step process (including friends of friends), etc. (Mitchell, 1969).

Reciprocity (also known as symmetry): a balance theory principle concerning the expectation that if A has a tie (such as friendship) with B, that tie will be reciprocated by B (i.e., B will be friends with A). The extent of reciprocity in a network can be assessed as the number of reciprocated ties divided by the number of dyads.

Similarity matrix: a type of adjacency matrix that shows, for all pairs of actors, how similar they are on a dimension. Similarity can be assessed by correlation coefficients, by counts or by other quantitative indicators. For example, each cell in the matrix could contain a correlation coefficient that summarized how similar two organizational actors were with respect to investments in 50 states.

Social capital: there are at least two, somewhat contradictory, meanings. At the individual level, social capital consists of the benefits that accrue to an actor as a result of the actor's social network connections (see Burt, 2000, for a review). At the communal level, social capital consists of 'civic spirit grounded on impartial application of the laws' (Portes, 2000; see also Putnam, 1996).

Social network: a set of actors and the relations (such as friendship, communication, advice) that connect them.

Social structure: the configuration of interactions that occur among the actors in a social system.

Sociogram: a picture in which actors are represented as points and relationships among actors are represented as lines in two-dimensional space.

Star: an actor who is at the centre of the social network in terms of popularity.

Strength of tie: this can be measured as a 'combination of the amount of time, the emotional intensity, the intimacy (mutual confiding), and the reciprocal services which characterize the tie' (Granovetter, 1973: 1361). Strong ties are those social relationships that are frequent, long-lasting and affect-laden (Krackhardt, 1992: 218–19), whereas weak ties are 'infrequent and distant' (Hansen, 1999: 84).

Structural hole: a gap between two actors or two clusters of actors (A and B) that can be spanned by another actor (C) who may, thereby, become the only member to belong to both A and B (if these are clusters), or who serves as the only intermediary between A and B. (See Burt, 1992, for more details).

Transitivity: a balance theory principle that concerns the expectation that relations among three actors will be complete. For example, if A regards both B and C as friends, there will be an expectation that B will also regard C as a friend, thus completing the transitive triple. The proportion of transitive triples in the network can be assessed as the number of completed transitive triples divided by the number of triples for which the addition of one missing link would make them complete.

Whole network: the complete set of ties among all actors in the network (as opposed to the egocentric network, which is the set of ties surrounding and including one actor in the network).

Workflow network: this represents the flow of work between individuals in the organization. For each individual in the organization, workflow network ties are with people who either provide or receive the individual's work (e.g., Mehra et al., 2001).

Zero block: a submatrix that contains no ties among the actors (see block).

Getting Started on Data Analysis and Interpretation

If your appetite is whetted for some hands-on investigation of the analysis of organizational social networks, we provide here a set of exercises followed by a detailed example that use concepts and procedures introduced in the book. Readers should pay particular attention to the specific steps involved, and also to the rationale behind the analysis and interpretation of the results. The example and exercises assume you have access to the UCINET (Borgatti et al., 1999) social network software package.

SOCIAL NETWORK EXERCISE 1: IMPORTING A DATA MATRIX AND USING MATRIX ALGEBRA

Many of the procedures in network analysis have their basis in graph theory. It is useful to know how to manipulate matrices in UCINET using graph theoretic ideas and matrix algebra methods. This exercise shows you how to create a data file, bring it into UCINET and perform a useful transformation on it.

Step One

You have surveyed the four partners of a law firm concerning who goes to whom for help and advice at work. In Table A.1 are the responses to your questionnaire (an 'x' means that the person reports going to the other person for advice).

Enter these data as a DL file in UCINET. This involves creating a square matrix (known as an adjacency matrix) to represent the data, preceded by 2 lines of preliminary information. The first row in the matrix will be person 1's responses and should look like this: 0 1 1 0. See the example in the UCINET user's guide. Save this as an MS Word file, and then save it as a text file. This will preserve formatting. Let us say we call the file 'Alba'.

Example of responses to a survey of law partners

(a) person 1:	(b) person 2:	(c) person 3:	(c) person 4:
1	1 x	1	1
2 x	2	2	2
3 x	3	3	3 x
4	4 x	4	4

Step Two

Import the text file you have saved as 'Alba' into UCINET. Go to Data, then Import, then DL. Type a: alba.txt.

Step Three

You want to discover how easy it is for the four partners to get advice from people through indirect contacts. As a first step, you decide to calculate how many paths of length 2 there are in the network. A path of length 2 is a path that goes from one actor to another actor through an intermediary: there are 2 steps.

To calculate all paths of length 2 in the matrix, do the following: use matrix multiplication to multiply the adjacency matrix by itself. Go to Tools, then Matrix Algebra. Type an equation of the following form: alba2 = prod(alba,alba)

Note: 'alba2' is the name you give to the output matrix that gives information on all paths of length 2. If you multiply this matrix by the original adjacency matrix, it will give you information on all paths of length 3 and so on.

Step Four

Display the results of your matrix multiplication of the adjacency matrix by itself. Go to Data, then Display, and type Alba2. Print the resulting matrix. This matrix tells you, for each pair of actors, how many paths of length 2 there are. For example, in Alba2, there should be a '2' in the cell located at row 2, column 3. This tells you that actor 2 can reach actor 3 by two different paths of length 2.

Step Five

Try to draw the paths between the four actors using the convention that a line with an arrowhead indicates direction. So, $1 \rightarrow 2$ means actor 1 goes to actor

3 for advice. Check to see that your drawing is compatible with your analysis of the number of '2' paths.

SOCIAL NETWORK
EXERCISE 2: COGNITIVE MAPS

In this exercise, we take a set of existing data on individuals' cognitive maps and create from these maps a representation of the 'actual' network. We then compare two individuals' cognitive maps with the 'actual' network to see if there is a significant overlap between perception and 'reality'. All the data are contained in UCINET.

Step One

We use data collected by David Krackhardt on friendship relations among managers in a high-tech company. In UCINET, go to DATA, DISPLAY, and type: KRACKFR Up will come the data. These data are discussed in Krackhardt and Kilduff (1999) – one of the articles discussed in this book.

Step Two

Note that there is a complete, asymmetric matrix for each of 21 actors. Read the brief discussion of the data set in Krackhardt and Kilduff (1999: 773) and what the data mean ('Perceived Friendship Network', 1999: 773). Make sure you understand how each respondent's matrix captures his or her cognitive map of the friendship network. See also the fuller description of individuals' cognitive maps in Kilduff and Krackhardt (1994: 91–2)

Step Three

We want to take the 21 cognitive maps and produce a version of the 'actual' network. The network software gives us several different ways to do this. To get a description of the possible choices, go to the UCINET help facility, INDEX, and type 'CSS'. This stands for 'cognitive social structures'. There are nine different choices of methods for producing an actual network from the perceived networks of individuals.

Let us assume we want to replicate what Kilduff and Krackhardt (1994: 92) did. Which of the nine methods of pooling data offered by UCINET will allow us to do this? Make a choice of one of the nine methods.

Step Four

Go to DATA, CSS, type KRACKFR for the input data set, choose a pooling method (the one you decided on in step three above), and run the analysis.

Step Five

You want to see how accurately the individuals in the data set perceive the network. Go to Data then Unpack. Type in Krackfr as the input data set. This will create data sets for each of the 21 people in Krackfr. Use QAP correlation to see how well two specific individuals' perceptions overlap with the actual network. (See the description of why QAP is necessary in Kilduff and Krackhardt, 1994. Go to Tools/Statistics/Matrix (QAP)/Correlation. Type in actor#20 for one data set and pooled for the other, and run the analysis. What is the Pearson correlation between the two data sets? Try this again with actor#5 and pooled – what is this correlation?

Step Six

As an optional extra, try exporting the pooled data set to the Krackplot network drawing software, using Data\Export\Krackplot. Use annealing for a layout method. If you've saved Krackplot in the same directory as UCINET then this should work, and you will be able to see the relative positions of actors 20 and 5. You can also use Netdraw (Borgatti, 2002) or one of the other network drawing software packages.

SOCIAL NETWORK EXERCISE 3: MEASURING STRUCTURAL HOLES

Given the excitement around the structural hole idea, the question arises: How can we best measure whether an actor spans across these holes in the network? Burt (1992) has introduced his own measure of structural constraint, whereas other researchers rely on Freeman's (1979) measure of betweenness. There is some confusion as to how these two measures relate to each other. This exercise explores this issue using the friendship network among the 14 men in the bank wiring room of the Hawthorne works.

Step One

In UCINET, go to 'Data/unpack' and input 'wiring'.

Step Two

Go to Network/centrality/Betweenness. Input 'RDPOS' – this is the friendship network from the Hawthorne works. The data is saved as FreemanBetweenness.

Step Three

Now go to Network/Ego Networks/Structural holes. Input 'RDPOS'. The output is saved as Holes.

Step Four

Go to Data/Join and choose the following data sets to be joined: Freeman-Betweenness and Holes. Run the analysis, making sure you choose 'column' as the basis for joining. Print the Joined matrix to see how the different actors fare on the different measures of how well they span across structural holes.

Step Five

Go to Tools/similarities and input 'joined' as the data set, and 'correlations' as the similarities to be calculated. Print the resulting correlation matrix.

Step Six

What do you conclude about the relationships between the measures? Which method appears to be most useful?

AN EXTENDED EXAMPLE OF HOW TO ANALYSE SOCIAL STRUCTURE ON THE FACTORY FLOOR

Here is an extended example of how to use social network analysis to answer questions about organizational behaviour. These data are from the UCINET data set RDGAM, a symmetric binary matrix. The example illustrates typical analytical procedures used in network analysis, and shows how to understand the output from these procedures.

Data Collection and Coding

Let us assume that a manager was recently assigned to a department consisting of 14 factory workers. These workers included Wiremen, Solderers and Inspectors, represented as Ws, Ss and Is, respectively, in the discussions below. The manager wanted to know how the 14 workers got along with each other. In particular, the manager wanted to know the answers to the following questions:

- 'Is there a specific pattern of social interactions among these workers?'
- 'Who is the most popular person in the department?'
- 'Who is the most influential person in this department?'

To begin answering these questions, the manager unobtrusively observed the workers during their breaks, watching who played cards and other games with whom. The manager coded the network data in a 14 by 14 matrix with column and row labels representing the different Wireworkers, Solderers and Inspectors. This is how the data looked (see Figure A.1).

In this matrix, '1' in a cell indicates that the actors in the corresponding row and column play games together, whereas a '0' indicates that no game-playing relationship exists between the row and column actors. For example, Inspector 1 (represented as 'I1') plays with worker W1, so the I1–W1 cell is recorded as '1'. In contrast, I1 does not play any games with W5, so the I1–W5 cell is recorded as '0'. This type of matrix is referred to as an adjacency matrix (or a sociomatrix) in network analysis. It contains information regarding the interactions of all the dyads in the network.

Data Display

The network data can also be presented in a graph called a sociogram. Using the KrackPlot software (Krackhardt et al., 1993), the manager prepared a sociogram of the game-playing relations among the fourteen workers (Figure A.2).

The sociogram suggests that there are two groups in the department connected by the bridging link between W5 and W7. The sociogram also shows that there are two isolates, I3 and S2, who do not play games with anyone in the department.

FIGURE A.1

	I1	I3	W1	W2	W3	W4	W5	W6	W7	W8	W9	S1	S2	S4
I1	0	0	1	1	1	1	0	0	0	0	0	0	0	0
I3	0	0	0	0	0	0	0	0	0	0	0	0	0	0
W1	1	0	0	1	1	1	1	0	0	0	0	1	0	0
W2	1	0	1	0	1	1	0	0	0	0	0	1	0	0
W3	1	0	1	1	0	1	1	0	0	0	0	1	0	0
W4	1	0	1	1	1	0	1	0	0	0	0	1	0	0
W5	0	0	1	0	1	1	0	0	1	0	0	1	0	0
W6	0	0	0	0	0	0	0	0	1	1	1	0	0	0
W7	0	0	0	0	0	0	1	1	0	1	1	0	0	1
W8	0	0	0	0	0	0	0	1	1	0	1	0	0	1
W9	0	0	0	0	0	0	0	1	1	1	0	0	0	1
S1	0	0	1	1	1	1	1	0	0	0	0	0	0	0
S2	0	0	0	0	0	0	0	0	0	0	0	0	0	0
S4	0	0	0	0	0	0	0	0	1	1	1	0	0	0

Adjacency matrix showing game-playing relations among 14 workers

FIGURE A.2

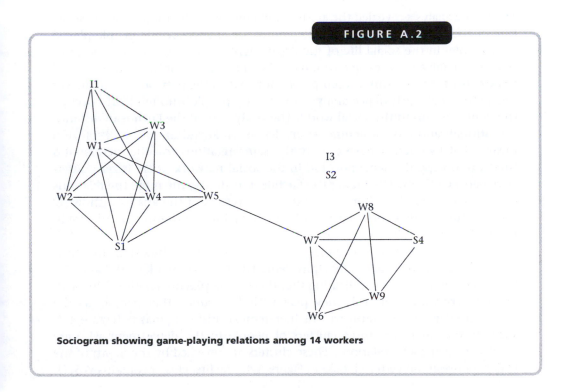

Sociogram showing game-playing relations among 14 workers

Clique Analysis

To obtain more specific information about sub-groups in the division, the manager ran clique analysis on the adjacency matrix and found five cliques, as follows.

Clique 1: I1 W1 W2 W3 W4
Clique 2: W1 W2 W3 W4 S1
Clique 3: W1 W3 W4 W5 S1
Clique 4: W6 W7 W8 W9
Clique 5: W7 W8 W9 S4

Each clique represents a cohesive sub-group, with every individual linked to every other individual. The results show that some workers belonged to more than one clique (for example, W7, W8, W9 belonged to cliques 4 and 5) and that some workers belonged to no cliques (I3 and S2).

Structural Equivalence

The clique analysis revealed the existence of cohesive sub-groups, but the structure of the network can also be analysed to see which specific people played similar roles in the social life of the department. According to the concept of structural equivalence, people who have the same or similar ties to others, tend to be equivalent in terms of their potential to act in the network. The manager ran a structural equivalence analysis to identify people who tended to occupy the same position in the social world. The analysis used the Euclidean distance operationalization of structural equivalence. A Euclidean distance of zero means that two actors have exactly the same relations to other actors, and therefore occupy the same position in the social network: there is zero difference between them. The higher the Euclidean distance, the more the relations of the two actors differ from each other. The results of the analysis, showing the structural equivalence matrix and the hierarchical clustering matrix, are in Figure A.3.

The structural equivalence matrix (Figure A.3) reports the extent to which two individuals are structurally equivalent. The two Wireworkers W3 and W4 have a cell entry of zero, indicating that their game-playing relationships with other workers are identical: they play with the same other people, as the sociogram (Figure A.2) confirms. The hierarchical clustering matrix (Figure A.4) suggests that there are three clusters of people in the department who are similar in their social relations. These clusters are revealed by the depth of the valleys between the vertical blocks in Figure A.4. The first cluster contains W5, I1, W2, W3, W1, W4 and S1, representing the left-hand group in Figure A.2. In this cluster, W5 is slightly different from the rest in the cluster (high Euclidean

FIGURE A.3

	I1	I3	W1	W2	W3	W4	W5	W6	W7	W8	W9	S1	S2	S4
I1	0.00	2.00	1.41	1.00	1.41	1.41	1.73	2.65	3.00	2.82	2.82	1.00	2.00	2.65
I3	2.00	0.00	2.45	2.24	2.45	2.45	2.24	1.73	2.24	2.00	2.00	2.24	0.00	1.73
W1	1.41	2.45	0.00	1.00	0.00	0.00	1.73	3.00	3.00	3.16	3.16	1.00	2.45	3.00
W2	1.00	2.24	1.00	0.00	1.00	1.00	1.41	2.83	3.16	3.00	3.00	1.41	2.24	2.83
W3	1.41	2.45	0.00	1.00	0.00	0.00	1.73	3.00	3.00	3.16	3.16	1.00	2.45	3.00
W4	1.41	2.45	0.00	1.00	0.00	0.00	1.73	3.00	3.00	3.16	3.16	1.00	2.45	3.00
W5	1.73	2.24	1.73	1.41	1.73	1.73	0.00	2.45	2.83	2.65	2.65	1.41	2.24	2.45
W6	2.65	1.73	3.00	2.83	3.00	3.00	2.45	0.00	1.41	1.00	1.00	2.83	1.73	0.00
W7	3.00	2.24	3.00	3.16	3.00	3.00	2.83	1.41	0.00	1.00	1.00	2.83	2.24	1.41
W8	2.83	2.00	3.16	3.00	3.16	3.16	2.65	1.00	1.00	0.00	0.00	3.00	2.00	1.00
W9	2.83	2.00	3.16	3.00	3.16	3.16	2.65	1.00	1.00	0.00	0.00	3.00	2.00	1.00
S1	1.00	2.24	1.00	1.41	1.00	1.00	1.41	2.83	2.83	3.00	3.00	0.00	2.24	2.83
S2	2.00	0.00	2.45	2.24	2.45	2.45	2.24	1.73	2.24	2.00	2.00	2.24	0.00	1.73
S4	2.65	1.73	3.00	2.83	3.00	3.00	2.45	0.00	1.41	1.00	1.00	2.83	1.73	0.00

Structural equivalence matrix showing Euclidean distances between all pairs

FIGURE A.4

```
        W I W W W W S I S W W W S
        5 1 2 3 1 4 1 3 2 7 9 8 6 4
Level
--------------------------------------------
0.000   .  .  .  XXXXX .  XXX .  XXX XXX
1.000   .  XXX XXXXXXX XXX XXXXX XXX
1.104   .  XXX XXXXXXX XXX XXXXXXXXX
1.217   .  XXXXXXXXXXX XXX XXXXXXXXX
1.543   XXXXXXXXXXXXX XXX XXXXXXXXX
1.855   XXXXXXXXXXXXX XXXXXXXXXXXXX
2.743   XXXXXXXXXXXXXXXXXXXXXXXXXXXX
```

Hierarchical clustering of the structural equivalence matrix

distances between W5 and others). The second cluster contains the isolated workers I3 and S2, who are equivalent in the sense of having no game-playing relations with others. The third cluster contains W7, W9, W8, W6 and S4, representing the right-hand group in Figure A.2.

The manager also ran an analysis using a different operationalization of structural equivalence, to check whether the structure revealed in the sociogram and in the Euclidean distance analyses was robust. CONCOR, which

```
            I W W W W W S  I  S W W W W S
            1 2 5 3 1 4 1  3  2 6 9 7 8 4
     Level
     ------------------------------------------
     2          XXXXX XXXXXXX XXX XXXXXXXXX
     1          XXXXXXXXXXXXX XXXXXXXXXXXXX
```

Partition diagram from CONCOR analysis on 14 workers

stands for CONvergence of iterated CORrelations, is a procedure that iteratively correlates the rows (or columns) of a matrix until all the entries in the matrix are either + 1 or – 1. The matrix can then be divided into two blocks with all the relations within blocks having the value of + 1, whereas the relations between blocks have the value of – 1 (see Wasserman and Faust, 1994: 376–81). The procedure can continue splitting each block into two blocks of equivalent actors at the discretion of the analyst. The CONCOR results for the current data set are presented in Figures A.5 and A.6.

The results in the partition diagram of Figure A.5 show that there are four sets of structurally equivalent actors. The first set contains I1, W2, W5 and the second set W3, W1, W4, S1. These two sets together comprise the grouping in the left-hand of the sociomatrix (Figure A.2). The third set of equivalent actors identified in the partition diagram is the set of isolates I3, S2. The fourth set contains W6, W9, W7, W8, S4, comprising the right-hand group in Figure A.2. The results are consistent with the previous analysis using Euclidean distance if we combine the first two sets of actors that CONCOR identified.

The results in Figure A.6 show structurally equivalent actors in the same block. Note that the information concerning game-playing relations in this matrix is the same as that in the original sociomatrix. By rearranging the order of the actors and permuting rows and columns in the original matrix, the blocked matrix allowed us to see clearly the relationships within and across groups of actors.

Centrality

The above analyses helped the manager understand the overall social structure of the department. The manager also wanted to know who the central players were in the division. To identify the central players in the network, the manager calculated two different centrality measures (degree and betweenness) for each worker in the division.

FIGURE A.6

	I1	W2	W5	W3	W1	W4	S1	I3	S2	W6	W9	W7	W8	S4
I1		1		1	1	1								
W2	1			1	1	1	1							
W5				1	1	1	1				1			
W3	1	1	1		1	1	1							
W1	1	1	1	1		1	1							
W4	1	1	1	1	1		1							
S1		1	1	1	1	1								
I3														
S2														
W6											1	1	1	
W9										1		1	1	1
W7				1						1	1		1	1
W8										1	1	1		1
S4											1	1	1	

Blocked matrix from CONCOR analysis on 14 workers

TABLE A.2

Table A.2   Output showing results of centrality analysis on 14 workers

	Degree	Normalized Degree		Betweenness	Normalized Betweenness
I1	4.000	30.769	I1	0.000	0.000
I3	0.000	0.000	I3	0.000	0.000
W1	6.000	46.154	W1	3.750	4.808
W2	5.000	38.462	W2	0.250	0.321
W3	6.000	46.154	W3	3.750	4.808
W4	6.000	46.154	W4	3.750	4.808
W5	5.000	38.462	W5	30.000	38.462
W6	3.000	23.077	W6	0.000	0.000
W7	5.000	38.462	W7	28.333	36.325
W8	4.000	30.769	W8	0.333	0.427
W9	4.000	30.769	W9	0.333	0.427
S1	5.000	38.462	S1	1.500	1.923
S2	0.000	0.000	S2	0.000	0.000
S4	3.000	23.077	S4	0.000	0.000

The results in Table A.2 show that W1, W3 and W4 have the highest degree centralities in the network: they played games with many other workers in the division. In the game-playing network, such individuals have many alternative partners with whom to play. The results also show that W5 and W7 have very high betweenness centrality scores. They were game-playing partners with people who did not play games with each other. Indeed, they served as bridges in the department, connecting different parts of the network together (as is displayed in Figure A.2).

This example demonstrates an extensive analysis of a well-known network data set (originally collected by Roethlisberger and Dickson (1939) and re-examined by Homans (1950)). More elaborate hypotheses could be constructed and more in-depth analysis could be performed if we located the actors in the specific cultural and historical contexts in which the data were collected.

Appendix 2

Analysing Cognitive Network Data Using MRQAP – A Methodological Note

One of the issues facing researchers who analyse social networks is that standard statistical tests may be inappropriate. Because the unit of observation is often the dyad, each unit in a data set may be dependent on other units. For example, in one study of social influence (Kilduff, 1992), 170 people provided data, but the independent and dependent matrices contained 28,730 observations on correlations between all possible pairs of people. These observations were clearly not independent because, for example, the correlation between John Smith and Ann Murray was not independent of the correlation between John Smith and Jim Stout (both observations contained the same data from John Smith). In statistical terms, the data may exhibit autocorrelation.

This autocorrelation problem particularly afflicts the analysis of cognitive networks. For example, in one test of the importance of perceived networks, the researchers created a matrix of indegree centrality ratings that included a row of 36 ratings from each of the 36 people in the organization. Each row in the matrix derived from the mind of a single individual, representing that individual's perception of how central the other individuals in the organization were. Thus each entry in a particular row exhibited systematic interdependence because it derived from the same source: the individual's cognitive map of the organization (Kilduff and Krackhardt, 1994).

Krackhardt (1988) showed that such row or column interdependence can positively bias ordinary-least-squares (OLS) tests, creating apparently significant relations between independent and dependent variables where no significant relationship in fact exists. One solution to the autocorrelation problem is to use non-parametric tests to determine whether independent variables are significant predictors of the dependent variable. The Multiple Regression Quadratic Assignment Procedure (MRQAP) allows one to do this.

MRQAP follows the logic established by QAP correlation. Basically, to decide if two matrices are significantly correlated, the rows and columns of one of the matrices are permuted to give a new matrix. This process is repeated an arbitrarily large number of times, such as 1,000. The result is a distribution of 1,000 correlations between two matrices. The actual correlation between the two matrices is compared to this reference distribution. If fewer than 5 per cent of the correlations derived from this reference distribution are larger than the observed correlation, the correlation between the two matrices is considered to be significant at the .05 level.

Extended to the regression situation, the procedure is similar. First, OLS regression coefficients are calculated in the usual manner. Then the rows and columns of the dependent variable matrix are permuted to give a new, mixed-up matrix. The OLS regression calculation is then repeated with the new dependent variable. This new regression produces different beta coefficients and overall R-squared values that are stored away. This permutation-regression process is repeated an arbitrarily large number of times. The distribution of the stored betas and R-squares for each of the independent variables under the set of permuted regressions becomes the reference distribution against which the observed original values are compared. If fewer than 5 per cent of the betas derived from the permuted regressions are larger than the observed beta, the beta is considered significant at the .05 level (1-tailed test).

Fortunately, the UCINET program can provide significant tests for correlations using the QAP method, and significant tests for beta coefficients using MRQAP. If you want to follow exactly the steps by which the significance of beta coefficients in a regression are calculated using this logic, then you can do so by following the method illustrated in Kilduff's (1990) analysis of the interpersonal structure of decision-making. Following Krackhardt (1988), Kilduff shows how the significance of beta coefficients in a regression can be estimated using QAP correlation and OLS regression in the case of autocorrelated data.

An application of this general approach was used to discover whether the self-monitoring personality variable moderated the effects of friendship networks on decision-making. At issue was whether high self-monitors (relative to low self-monitors) tended to be more influenced by their friends when making important decisions. The correlation was higher for the high self-monitors than for the low self-monitors between two matrices showing friendship links and decision similarity. Was this difference in correlations significant? Individuals were randomly assigned to the two categories of high and low self-monitors, the correlations were recalculated, this process was repeated 10,000 times with the difference in correlations saved to a file. Then the observed difference in correlations was compared with the distribution of all possible differences. This Random Assignment Procedure (RAP) showed that the observed difference was significant at the .05 level in support of the hypothesis that high self-monitors (compared to low self-monitors) tended to be more influenced in their decision-making by their friends (Kilduff, 1992).

References

Abell, P. 1987. *The syntax of social life: The theory and method of comparative narratives.* New York: Clarendon Press.

Adams, B.N. and Sydie, R.A. 2001. *Sociological theory.* Thousand Oaks, CA: Pine Forge Press.

Adorno, T.W., Frenkel-Brunswik, E., Levinson, D.J. and Stanford, R.N. 1950. *The authoritarian personality.* New York: Harper & Row.

Agnew, C.R., Loving, T.J. and Drigotas, S.M. 2001. Substituting the forest for the trees: Social networks and the prediction of romantic relationship state and fate. *Journal of Personality and Social Psychology*, 81: 1042–57.

Alba, R.D. 1982. Taking stock of network analysis: A decade's results. *Research in the Sociology of Organizations*, 1: 39–74.

Allen, T.J. and Cohen, S.I. 1969. Information flow in research and development laboratories. *Administrative Science Quarterly*, 14: 12–19.

Andrews, S.B. and Knoke, D. (eds). 1999. Networks in and around organizations. *Research in the Sociology of Organizations*, 16.

Baker, W.E. 1990. Market networks and corporate behavior. *American Journal of Sociology*, 96: 589–625.

Baker, W.E. 1994. *Networking smart.* New York: McGraw-Hill.

Baker, W.E. 2000. *Achieving success through social capital.* San Francisco: Jossey-Bass.

Baker, W.E. and Faulkner, R.R. 1993. The social organization of conspiracy: Illegal networks in the heavy electrical equipment industry. *American Sociological Review*, 58: 837–60.

Baker, W.E. and Faulkner, R.R. 2002. Interorganizational networks. In J.A.C. Baum (ed.), *The Blackwell companion to organizations*, pp. 520–40. Oxford: Blackwell.

Barker, J.R. 1993. Tightening the iron cage: Concertive control in self-managing teams. *Administrative Science Quarterly*, 38: 408–37.

Barley, S.R. 1990. The alignment of technology and structure through roles and networks. *Administrative Science Quarterly*, 35: 61–103.

Barley, S.R., Meyer, G.W. and Gash, D.C. 1988. Cultures of culture: Academics, practitioners, and the pragmatics of normative control. *Administrative Science Quarterly*, 33: 24–60.

Barnes, J.A. 1979. Network analysis: Orienting notion, rigorous technique or substantive field of study? In P.W. Holland and S. Leinhardt (eds), *Perspectives on social network research*, pp. 403–23. New York: Academic Press.

Baron, R.A. 1989. Personality and organizational conflict: Effects of the type A behavior pattern and self-monitoring. *Organizational Behavior and Human Decision Processes*, 44: 196–281.

Baum, J.A.C. 2002. *Companion to organizations*. Maldon, MA: Blackwell.

Baum, J.A.C. and Singh, J.V. 1994. *Evolutionary dynamics of organizations*. Oxford: Oxford University Press.

Becker, G. 1976. *The economic approach to human behavior*. Chicago: University of Chicago Press.

Benson, K. 1975. The interorganizational network as a political economy. *Administrative Science Quarterly*, 20: 229–49.

Berkman, L.F. and Syme, L. 1979. Social networks, host resistance, and mortality: A nine-year follow-up study of Alameda County residents. *American Journal of Epidemiology*, 109: 186–204.

Berkowitz, S.D. 1982. *An introduction to structural analysis*. Toronto: Butterworth.

Berscheid, E., Graziano, W.G., Monson, T. and Dermer, M. 1976. Outcome dependency: Attention, attribution, and attraction. *Journal of Personality and Social Psychology*, 34: 978–989.

Blau, P.M. 1964. *Exchange and power in social life*. New York: John Wiley.

Blau, P.M. 1977. *Inequality and heterogeneity: A primitive theory of social structure*. New York: Free Press.

Blau, P.M. 1984. *Crosscutting social circles: Testing a macrostructural theory of intergroup relations*. Orlando, FL: Academic Press.

Boissevain, J. 1973. An exploration of two first-order zones. In J. Boissevain and J.C. Mitchell (eds), *Network analysis studies in human interaction*, pp. 125–48. The Hague: Mouton.

Boissevain, J. 1979. Network analysis: A reappraisal. *Current Anthropology*, 20: 392–4.

Bolino, M.C., Turnley, W.H. and Bloodgood, J.M. 2002. Citizenship behavior and the creation of social capital in organizations. *Academy of Management Review*, 27: 505–22.

Bonacich, P. 1987. Power and centrality: A family of measures. *American Journal of Sociology*, 92: 1170–82.

Boorman, S.A. and White, H.C. 1976. Social structure from multiple networks II: Role structures. *American Journal of Sociology*, 81: 1384–446.

Borgatti, S.P. 2002. *Netdraw visualization software*. Cambridge, MA: Analytic Technologies.

Borgatti, S.P., Everett, M.G. and Freeman, L.C. 1999. *UCINET 5 for Windows*. Columbia, SC: Analytic Technologies.

Bossard, J.H.S. 1945. The law of family interaction. *American Journal of Sociology*, 50: 292–4.

Bott, E. 1957. *Family and social network: Roles, norms, and external relationships in ordinary urban families*. London: Tavistock.

Bougon, M.G., Weick, K.E. and Binkhorst, D. 1977. Cognition in organizations: An analysis of the Utrecht Jazz Orchestra. *Administrative Science Quarterly*, 22: 606–39.

Bourdieu, P. 1980. Le capital social: Notes provisoires. *Actes de la Recherche en Sciences Sociales*, 3: 2–3.

Brass, D.J. 1984. Being in the right place: A structural analysis of individual influence in an organization. *Administrative Science Quarterly*, 29: 519–39.

Brass, D.J. 1985. Men's and women's networks: A study of interaction patterns and influence in organizations. *Academy of Management Journal*, 28: 327–43.

Brass, D.J. 1995. A social network perspective on human resources management. In Gerald R. Ferris (ed.), *Research in personnel and human resources management*, 13: 39–79. Greenwich, CT: JAI Press.

Brass, D.J. and Labianca, G. 1999. Social capital, social liabilities, and social resources management. In R.T.A.J. Leenders and S.M. Gabbay (eds), *Corporate social capital and liability*, pp. 323–38.

Breiger, R.L. 1974. The duality of persons and groups. *Social Forces*, 53: 181–90.

Breiger, R.L. 2000. A tool kit for practice theory. *Poetics*, 27: 91–115.

Breiger, R.L. 2002. Poststructuralism in organizational studies. *Research in the Sociology of Organizations*, 19: 295–305.

Breiger, R.L., Boorman, S.A. and Arabie, P. 1975. An algorithm for clustering relational data with application to social network analysis and comparison with multidimensional scaling. *Journal of Mathematical Psychology*, 12: 328–83.

Breiger, R.L. and Ennis, J.G. 1979. Personae and social roles: The network structure of personality types in small groups. *Social Psychology Quarterly*, 42: 262–70.

Brown, J.S. and Duguid, P. 2000. *The social life of information*. Cambridge, MA: Harvard University Press.

Bryson, G. 1945. *Man and society: The Scottish inquiry of the eighteenth century*. Princeton, NJ: Princeton University Press.

Burt, R.S. 1978. Cohesion versus structural equivalence as a basis for network subgroups. *Sociological Methods and Research*, 7: 189–212.

Burt, R.S. 1982. *Toward a structural theory of action*. New York: Academic Press.

Burt, R.S. 1983. *Corporate profits and cooptation*. New York: Academic Press.

Burt, R.S. 1987. Social contagion and innovation: Cohesion versus structural equivalence. *American Journal of Sociology*, 92: 1287–335.

Burt, R.S. 1992. *Structural holes: The social structure of competition*. Cambridge, MA: Harvard University Press.

Burt, R.S. 2000. The network structure of social capital. *Research in Organizational Behavior*, 22: 345–423.

Burt, R.S. 2002. Bridge decay. *Social Networks*, 24: 333–63.

Burt, R.S. and Ronchi, D. 1990. Contested control in a large manufacturing plant. In J. Wessie and H. Flap (eds), *Social networks through time*, pp. 121–57. Utrecht, Netherlands: ISOR.

Carley, K.M. 1999. On the evolution of social and organizational networks. *Research in the Sociology of Organizations*, 16: 3–30.

Carley, K.M. and Prietula, M.J. (eds). 1994. *Computational organizational theory*. Hillsdale, NJ: Erlbaum.

Cartwright, D. and Harary, F. 1956. Structural balance: A generalization of Heider's theory. *Psychological Review*, 63: 277–92.

Cassell, J. 1996. The woman in the surgeon's body: Understanding difference. *American Anthropologist*, 98: 41–53.

Cialdini, R.B. 1989. Indirect tactics of impression management: Beyond basking. In R.A. Giacalone and P. Rosenfeld (eds), *Impression management in the organization*, pp. 45–56. Hillsdale, NJ: Erlbaum.

Clifford, J. and Marcus, G.E. 1986. *Writing culture: The poetics and politics of ethnography*. Berkeley, CA: University of California Press.

Cohen, S., Doyle, W.J., Skoner, D.P., Rabin, B.S. and Gwaltney, J.M. 1997. Social ties and susceptibility to the common cold. *Journal of the American Medical Association*, 277: 1940–44.

Coleman, J.S. 1990. *Foundations of social theory*. Cambridge, MA: Harvard University Press.

Coleman, J.S., Katz, E. and Menzel, H. 1966. *Medical innovation: A diffusion study*. New York: Bobbs-Merrill.

Crockett, W.H. 1982. Balance, agreement, and positivity in the cognition of small social structures. *Advances in Experimental Social Psychology*, 15: 1–57.

Cyert, R.M. and March, J.G. 1963. *A behavioral theory of the firm*. Englewood Cliffs, NJ: Prentice-Hall.

D'Andrade, R.G. 1992. Schemas and motivation. In R.G. D'Andrade and C. Strauss (eds), *Human motives and cultural models*, pp. 23–44. Cambridge: Cambridge University Press.

Davis, A., Gardner, B.B. and Gardner, M.R. 1941. *Deep south: A social anthropological study of caste and class*. Chicago: University of Chicago Press.

Davis, G.F. 1991. Agents without principles? The spread of the poison pill through the intercorporate network. *Administrative Science Quarterly*, 36: 583–613.

Davis, G.F. and Mizuhi, M.S. 1999. The money center cannot hold: Commercial banks in the US system of governance. *Administrative Science Quarterly*, 44: 215–39.

Davis, J.A. 1963. Structural balance, mechanical solidarity, and interpersonal relations. *American Journal of Sociology*, 68: 444–62.

Davis, J.A. 1979. The Davis/Holland/Leinhardt studies: An overview. In P.W. Holland and S. Leinhardt (eds), *Perspectives on social network research*, pp. 51–62. New York: Academic Press.

Dawes, R. 1976. Shallow psychology. In J. Carroll and J. Payne (eds), *Cognition and social behavior*, pp. 3–12. Hillsdale, NJ: Erlbaum.

De Saussure, F. 1939. *Course in general linguistics*. New York: Philosophy Library.

De Sola Pool, I. and Kochen, M. 1978. Contacts and influence. *Social networks*, 1: 5–51.

De Soto, C.B. 1960. Learning a social structure. *Journal of Abnormal and Social Psychology*, 60: 417–21.

Degenne, A. and Forse, M. 1999. *Introducing social networks*. London: Sage.

Derrida, J. 1976. *Of grammatology*. Baltimore, MD: Johns Hopkins University Press.

Digman, J.M. 1990. Personality structure: Emergence of the five-factor model. *Annual Review of Psychology*, 41: 417–40.

DiMaggio, P. (ed.). 2001. *The twenty-first-century firm: Changing economic organization in international perspective.* Princeton, NJ: Princeton University Press.

DiMaggio, P.J. and Powell, W.W. 1983. The iron cage revisited: Institutional isomorphism and collective rationality in organizational fields. *American Sociological Review,* 48: 147–60.

Doreian, P. 2002. Event sequences as generators of social network evolution. *Social Networks,* 24: 93–119.

Doreian, P., Kapuscinski, R., Krackhardt, D. and Szczypula, J. 1996. A brief history of balance through time. *Journal of Mathematical Sociology,* 21: 113–31.

Dorst, J.D. 1989. *The written suburb: An American site, an ethnographic dilemma.* Philadelphia: University of Pennsylvania Press.

Dyer, J.H. and Singh, H. 1998. The relational view: Cooperative strategy and sources of interorganizational competitive advantage. *Academy of Management Journal,* 23: 660–79.

Eisenhardt, K. and Bhatia, L. 2002. Organizational computation and complexity. In J.A.C. Baum (ed.), *Companion to organizations,* pp. 442–66. Oxford: Blackwell.

Emery, F.E. and Trist, E.L. 1965. The causal structure of organizational environments. *Human Relations,* 18: 21–32.

Emirbayer, M. and Goodwin, J. 1994. Network analysis, culture, and the problem of agency. *American Journal of Sociology,* 99: 1411–54.

Erickson, B.H. 1988. The relational basis of attitudes. In B. Wellman and S.D. Berkowitz (eds), *Social structures: A network approach,* pp. 99–121. Cambridge: Cambridge University Press.

Erlich, D., Guttman, I., Schonbach, P. and Mills, J. 1957. Post-decision exposure to relevant information. *Journal of Abnormal and Social Psychology,* 54: 98–102.

Fernandez, R.M. and Gould, R.V. 1994. A dilemma of state power: Brokerage and influence in the national health policy domain. *American Journal of Sociology,* 99: 1455–91.

Fernandez, R.M. and Weinberg, N. 1997. Sifting and sorting: Personal contacts and hiring in a retail bank. *American Sociological Review,* 62: 883–902.

Festinger, L. 1949. The analysis of sociograms using matrix algebra. *Human Relations,* 2: 153–58.

Festinger, L. 1954. A theory of social comparison processes. *Human Relations,* 7: 117–40.

Festinger, L. and Hutte, H.A. 1954. An experimental investigation of the effect of unstable interpersonal relations in a group. *Journal of Abnormal and Social Psychology,* 49: 513–23.

Festinger, L., Schachter, S. and Back, K.W. 1950. *Social pressures in informal groups: A study of human factors in housing.* New York: Harper.

Fish, S. 1980. *Is there a text in this class: The authority of interpretive communities.* Cambridge, MA: Harvard University Press.

Fiske, A.P. 1992. The four elementary forms of sociality: Framework for a unified theory of social relations. *Psychological Review,* 99: 689–723.

Flap, H., Bulder, B. and Volker, B. 1998. Intra-organizational networks and performance. *Computational and Mathematical Organization Theory,* 4: 109–47.

Forsyth, E. and Katz, L. 1946. A matrix approach to the analysis of sociometric data: Preliminary report. *Sociometry*, 9: 340–7.

Freeman, L.C. 1979. Centrality in social networks: I. Conceptual clarification. *Social Networks*, 1: 215–39.

Freeman, L.C. 1992. Filling in the blanks: A theory of cognitive categories and the structure of social affiliation. *Social Psychology Quarterly*, 55: 118–27.

Friedkin, N. 1998. *A structural theory of social influence.* Cambridge: Cambridge University Press.

Friedman, R.A. 1996. Defining the scope and logic of minority and female network groups: Can separation enhance integration? *Research in Personnel and Human Resource Management*, 14: 307–49.

Galaskiewicz, J. 1985. *Social organization of an urban grants economy.* New York: Academic Press.

Galaskiewicz, J. 1996. The 'new network analysis' and its application to organizational theory and behavior. In D. Iacobucci (ed.), *Networks and marketing*, pp. 19–31. Thousand Oaks, CA: Sage.

Gangestad, S. 1984. On the etiology of individual differences in self-monitoring and expressive control: Testing the case of strong genetic influence. Unpublished doctoral dissertation, Psychology Department, University of Minnesota.

Gangestad, S. and Snyder, M. 1985. On the nature of self-monitoring: An examination of latent causal structure. *Review of Personality and Social Psychology*, 6: 65–85.

Gergen, K.J. 1990. Toward a postmodern psychology. *The Humanistic Psychologist*, 18: 23–43.

Ghoshal, S. and Bartlett, C.A. 1990. The multinational corporation as an interorganizational network. *Academy of Management Review*, 15: 603–25.

Ghoshal, S. and Moran, P. 1996. Bad for practice: A critique of the transaction cost theory. *Academy of Management Review*, 21: 31–48.

Giddens, A. 1984. *The constitution of society: Outline of the theory of structuration.* Berkeley, CA: University of California Press.

Giroux, H.A. 1992. *Border crossings: Cultural workers and the politics of education.* New York: Routledge.

Gladwell, M. 2000. *The tipping point: How little things can make a big difference.* Boston: Little, Brown.

Gluckman, M. 1967. *Ideas in Barotse jurisprudence.* Manchester: Manchester University Press.

Goethals, G.R. and Darley, J.M. 1987. Social comparison theory: Self-evaluation and group life. In B. Mullen and G.R. Goethals (eds), *Theories of group behavior*, pp. 21–47. New York: Springer-Verlag.

Goffman, E. 1959. *The presentation of self in everyday life.* Garden City, NY: Doubleday.

Goffman, E. 1961. *Asylums: Essays on the social situation of mental patients and other inmates.* New York: Anchor.

Gouldner, A.W. 1960. The norm of reciprocity: A preliminary statement. *American Sociological Review*, 25: 161–79.

Grandori, A. (ed.). 1999. *Interfirm networks: Organization and industrial competitiveness.* London: Routledge.

Granovetter, M. 1973. The strength of weak ties. *American Journal of Sociology*, 78: 1360–80.

Granovetter, M. 1974. *Getting a job: A study of contacts and careers.* Chicago: University of Chicago Press.

Granovetter, M. 1979. The theory gap in social network analysis. In P.W. Holland and S. Leinhardt (eds), *Perspectives on social network research*, pp. 501–18.

Granovetter, M. 1982. The strength of weak ties: A network theory revisited. In P. Marsden and N. Lin (eds), *Social structural and network analysis*, pp. 130–50. Beverly Hills, CA: Sage.

Granovetter, M.S. 1985. Economic action and social structure: The problem of embeddedness. *American Journal of Sociology*, 91: 481–510.

Granovetter, M. 1995. *Getting a job: A study of contacts and careers.* 2nd edn. Chicago: University of Chicago Press.

Grant, R. 1996. Toward a knowledge-based theory of the firm. *Strategic Management Journal*, 17: 109–22.

Gulati, R. 1995. Social structure and alliance formation patterns: A longitudinal analysis. *Administrative Science Quarterly*, 40: 619–52.

Gulati, R., Dialdin, D.A. and Wang, L. 2002. Organizational networks. In J.A.C. Baum (ed.), *The Blackwell companion to organizations*, pp. 281–303. Oxford: Blackwell.

Gulati, R. and Gargiulo, M. 1999. Where do interorganizational networks come from? *American Journal of Sociology*, 104: 1439–93.

Hage, P. and Harary, F. 1996. *Island networks: Communication, kinship and classification structures in Oceania.* Cambridge: Cambridge University Press.

Hambrick, D.C. 1994. What if the Academy actually mattered? *Academy of Management Review*, 19: 11–16.

Hamel, G., Doz, Y.L. and Prahalad, C.K. 1989. Collaborate with your competitors – and win. *Harvard Business Review*, 67 (1): 133–9.

Hannan, M.T. and Freeman, J. 1977. The population ecology of organizations. *American Journal of Sociology*, 82: 929–64.

Hansen, M.T. 1999. The search-transfer problem: The role of weak ties in sharing knowledge across organizational subunits. *Administrative Science Quarterly*, 44: 82–111.

Harary, F., Norman, R.Z. and Cartwright, D. 1965. *Structural models: An introduction to the theory of directed graphs.* New York: Wiley.

Harrison, J.R. and Carroll, G.R. 1991. Keeping the faith: A model of cultural transmission in formal organizations. *Administrative Science Quarterly*, 36: 552–82.

Heider, F. 1958. *The psychology of interpersonal relations.* New York: Wiley.

Helgesen, S. 1995. *The web of inclusion: A new architecture for building great organizations.* New York: Doubleday.

Holland, P.W. and Leinhardt, S. 1977. Transitivity in structural models of small groups. In S. Leinhardt (ed.), *Social networks: A developing paradigm*, pp. 49–66. New York: Academic Press.

Homans, G.C. 1950. *The human group*. New York: Harcourt, Brace and World.

Hosch, H.M., Leippe, M.R., Marchioni, P.M. and Cooper, D.S. 1984. Victimization, self-monitoring, and eye-witness identification. *Journal of Applied Psychology*, 69: 280–8.

Huber, J. (ed.). 1991. *Macro-micro linkages in sociology*. Newbury Park, CA: Sage.

Human, S.E. and Provan, K.G. 2000. Legitimacy building in the evolution of small-firm multilateral networks: A comparative study of success and demise. *Administrative Science Quarterly*, 45: 327–65.

Hummon, N.P. and Carley, K. 1993. Social networks as normal science. *Social Networks*, 15: 71–106.

Hummon, N.P. and Fararo, T.J. 1995. Actors and networks as objects. *Social Networks*, 17: 1–26.

Ibarra, H. 1992. Homophily and differential returns: Sex differences in network structure and access in an advertising firm. *Administrative Science Quarterly*, 37: 422–47.

Janicik, G.A. 2000. Coordination across structural holes: Examining the learning of relations. Unpublished manuscript, Management Department, New York University.

Jenkins, J.M. 1993 Self-monitoring and turnover: The impact of personality on intent to leave. *Journal of Organizational Behavior*, 14: 83–9.

Johnson, J.C. and Orbach, M.K. 2002. Perceiving the political landscape: Ego biases in cognitive political networks. *Social Networks*, 24: 291–310.

Johnson, K. 1996. Divorced from the job, still wedded to the culture. *New York Times*, 16 June: F11.

Jones, E.E. and Baumeister, R. 1976. The self-monitor looks at the ingratiator. *Journal of Personality and Social Psychology*, 44: 654–74.

Kadushin, C. 1966. The friends and supporters of psychotherapy: On social circles in urban life. *American Sociological Review*, 31: 685–99.

Kadushin, C. 1995. Friendship among the French financial elite. *American Sociological Review*, 60: 202–21.

Kahneman, D. and Tversky, A. 1979. Prospect theory: An analysis of decision under risk. *Econometrica*, 47: 263–91.

Kapferer, B. 1972. *Strategy and transaction in an African factory*. Manchester: University of Manchester Press.

Kilduff, M. 1990. The interpersonal structure of decision-making: A social comparison approach to organizational choice. *Organizational Behavior and Human Decision Processes*, 47: 270–88.

Kilduff, M. 1992. The friendship network as a decision-making resource: Dispositional moderators of social influences on organizational choice. *Journal of Personality and Social Psychology*, 62: 168–80.

Kilduff, M. 1993. Deconstructing organizations. *Academy of Management Review*, 18: 13–31.

Kilduff, M. and Day, D.V. 1994. Do chameleons get ahead? The effects of self-monitoring on managerial careers. *Academy of Management Journal*, 37: 1047–60.

Kilduff, M. and Kelemen, M. 2001. The consolations of organization theory. *British Journal of Management*, 12: 55–9.

Kilduff, M. and Krackhardt, D. 1994. Bringing the individual back in: A structural analysis of the internal market for reputation in organizations. *Academy of Management Journal*, 37: 87–108.

Kilduff, M. and Mehra, A. 1997. Postmodernism and organizational research. *Academy of Management Review*, 22: 453–81.

Kilduff, M. and Oh, H. 2002. Deconstructing diffusion: A case study in the sociology of knowledge. Working paper, Smeal College of Business Administration, Pennsylvania State University.

Knoke, D. and Kuklinski, J.H. 1982. *Network analysis*. Beverly Hills, CA: Sage.

Kogut, B. 2000. The network as knowledge: Generative rules and the emergence of structure. *Strategic Management Journal*, 21: 405–25.

Kondo, D.K. 1990. *Crafting selves: Power, gender and discourses of identity in a Japanese workplace*. Chicago: University of Chicago Press.

Krackhardt, D. 1987. Cognitive social structures. *Social Networks*, 9: 109–34.

Krackhardt, D. 1988. Predicting with networks: Nonparametric multiple regression analysis of dyadic data. *Social Networks*, 10: 359–81.

Krackhardt, D. 1990. Assessing the political landscape: Structure, cognition and power in organizations. *Administrative Science Quarterly*, 35: 342–69.

Krackhardt, D. 1992. The strength of strong ties: The importance of *Philos* in organizations. In N. Nohria and R.G. Eccles (eds), *Networks and organizations*, pp. 216–39.

Krackhardt, D. 1994. Graph theoretical dimensions of informal organizations. In K. Carley and M. Prietula (eds), *Computational organizational theory*, pp. 89–111. Hillsdale, NJ: Erlbaum.

Krackhardt, D. 1998. Simmelian ties: Super strong and sticky. In R. Kramer and M. Neale (eds), *Power and influence in organizations*, pp. 21–38. Thousand Oaks, CA: Sage.

Krackhardt, D. 1999. The ties that torture: Simmelian tie analysis in organizations. *Research in the Sociology of Organizations*, 16: 183–210.

Krackhardt, D. and Brass, D.J. 1994. Intraorganizational networks: The micro side. In S. Wasserman and J. Galaskiewicz (eds), *Advances in social network analysis*, pp. 207–29. Thousand Oaks, CA: Sage.

Krackhardt, D. and Hanson, J. 1993. Informal networks: The company behind the chart. *Harvard Business Review*, 71 (4): 104–11.

Krackhardt, D. and Kilduff, M. 1990. Friendship patterns and culture: The control of organizational diversity. *American Anthropologist*, 92: 142–5.

Krackhardt, D. and Kilduff, M. 1999. Whether close or far: Social distance effects on perceived balance in friendship networks. *Journal of Personality and Social Psychology*, 76: 770–82.

Krackhardt, D. and Kilduff, M. 2002. Structure, culture and Simmelian ties in entrepreneurial firms. *Social Networks*, 24: 279–90.

Krackhardt, D., Lundberg, M. and O'Rourke, L. 1993. KrackPlot: A picture's worth a thousand words. *Connections*, 16 (1 & 2): 37–47.

Krackhardt, D. and Porter, L.T. 1985. When friends leave: A structural analysis of the relationship between turnover and stayers' attitudes. *Administrative Science Quarterly*, 30: 242–61.

Krachkardt, D. and Porter, L.T. 1986. The snowball effect: Turnover embedded in communication networks. *Journal of Applied Psychology*, 71: 1–6.

Kuethe, J.L. 1962. Social schemas. *Journal of Abnormal and Social Psychology*, 64: 31–8.

Kumbasar, E.A., Romney, K. and Batchelder, W.H. 1994. Systematic biases in social perception. *American Journal of Sociology*, 100: 477–505.

Kunda, G. 1992. *Engineering culture: Control and commitment in a high-tech corporation*. Philadelphia: Temple University Press.

Lacan, J. 1968. *The language of the self: The function of language in psychoanalysis*. Baltimore, MD: Johns Hopkins University Press.

Larson, A. 1992. Network dyads in entrepreneurial settings: A study of the governance of exchange relations. *Administrative Science Quarterly*, 37: 76–104.

Latour, B. 1987. *Science in action: How to follow scientists and engineers through society*. Cambridge, MA: Harvard University Press.

Leenders, R. and Gabbay, S.M. (eds). 1999. *Corporate social capital and liability*. Norwell, MA: Kluwer.

Leinhardt, S. (ed.). 1977. *Social networks: A developing paradigm*. New York: Academic Press.

Lévi-Strauss, C. 1963. *Structural anthropology*. New York: Basic Books.

Lewin, K. 1951. *Field theory in social science: Selected theoretical papers*. New York: Harper.

Lincoln, J.R. and Miller, J. 1979. Work and friendship ties in organizations: A comparative analysis of relational networks. *Administrative Science Quarterly*, 24: 181–99.

Lipset, S.M., Trow, M.A. and Coleman, J.S. 1956. *Union democracy: The internal politics of the International Typographical Union*. Garden City, NY: Anchor Books.

Lorrain, F. and White, H.C. 1971. Structural equivalence of individuals in social networks. *Journal of Mathematical Sociology*, 1: 49–80.

Luce, R.D. and Perry, A.D. 1949. A method of matrix analysis of group structure. *Psychometrika*, 14: 95–116.

Lyotard, J.F. 1984. *The post-modern condition: A report on knowledge*. Minneapolis: University of Minnesota Press.

McClelland, D. 1961. *The achieving society*. New York: Free Press.

McPherson, J.M., Popielarz, P.A. and Drobnic, S. 1992. Social networks and organizational dynamics. *American Sociological Review*, 57: 153–70.

McPherson, M., Smith-Lovin, L. and Cook, J.M. 2001. Birds of a feather: Homophily in social networks. *Annual Review of Sociology*, 27: 415–44.

Mandler, J.M. 1979. Categorical and schematic organization in memory. In C.R. Puff (ed.), *Memory organization and structure*, pp. 259–99. New York: Academic Press.

March, J.G. and Simon, H.A. 1958. *Organizations*. New York: Wiley.

Mark, N. 1998. Beyond individual differences: Social differentiation from first principles. *American Sociological Review*, 63: 309–30.

Marsden, P.V. and Friedkin, N. 1993. Network studies of social influence. *Sociological Methods and Research*, 22: 127–51.

Marsden, P.V. and Podolny, J. 1990. Dynamic analysis of network diffusion processes. In J. Wessie and H. Flap (eds), *Social networks through time*, pp. 197–214. Utrecht, Netherlands: ISOR.

Mayhew, B.H. 1980. Structuralism versus individualism. Part 1: Shadow boxing in the dark. *Social Forces*, 59: 335–75.

Mead, G.H. 1934. *Mind, self and society*. Chicago: University of Chicago Press.

Mehra, A., Dixon, A.L., Robertson, B. and Brass, D.J. 2002. The external and internal social capital of unit leaders: Implications for performance in multiunit organizations. Working paper, University of Cincinnati.

Mehra, A., Kilduff, M. and Brass, D.J. 1998. At the margins: A distinctiveness approach to the social identity and social networks of under-represented groups. *Academy of Management Journal*, 41: 441–52.

Mehra, A., Kilduff, M. and Brass, D.J. 2001. The social networks of high and low self-monitors: Implications for workplace performance. *Administrative Science Quarterly*, 35: 121–46.

Merton, R.K. 1957. *Social theory and social structure*. Glencoe, IL: Free Press.

Michaelson, A. and Contractor, N.S. 1992. Structural position and perceived similarity. *Social Psychology Quarterly*, 55: 300–10.

Michels, R. 1962. *Political parties: A sociological study of the oligarchical tendencies of modern democracy*. New York: Free Press.

Mitchell, J.C. 1969. *Social networks in urban settings*. Manchester: Manchester University Press.

Mitchell, J.C. 1974. Social networks. *Annual Review of Anthropology*, 3: 279–99.

Mizruchi, M.S. 1994. Social network analysis: Recent achievements and current controversies. *Acta Sociologica*, 37: 329–43.

Mizruchi, M.S. and Fein, L.C. 1999. The social construction of organizational knowledge: A study of the uses of coercive, mimetic, and normative isomorphism. *Administrative Science Quarterly*, 44: 653–83.

Monge, P.R. and Contractor, N.S. 1999. Emergence of communication networks. In F.M. Jablin and L.I. Putnam (eds), *The new handbook of organizational communication: Advances in theory, research, and methods*, pp. 440–502. Thousand Oaks, CA: Sage.

Murnighan, J.K. and Brass, D.J. 1991. Intraorganizational coalitions. *Research on Negotiations in Organizations*, 3: 283–307.

Nadel, S.F. 1957. *The theory of social structure*. New York: Free Press.

Nelson, J.I. 1966. Clique contacts and family orientations. *American Sociological Review*, 31: 663–72.

Nelson, R.E. 1989. The strength of strong ties: Social networks and intergroup conflict in organizations. *Academy of Management Journal*, 32: 377–401.

Newcomb, T.M. 1961. *The acquaintance process*. New York: Holt, Rinehart & Winston.

Nohria, N. and Eccles, R.G. (eds). 1992. *Networks and organizations: Structure, form and action*. Boston, MA: Harvard Business School Press.

Nohria, N. and Ghoshal, S. 1997. *The differentiated network: A new model for organizing multinational corporations*. San Francisco: Jossey-Bass.

Nooteboom, B. 1999. *Inter-firm alliances: Analysis and design*. London: Routledge.

Oh, H., Kilduff, M. and Brass, D.J. 2002. Social personality and social capital. Working paper, Management Department, Hong Kong University of Science and Technology.

Oliver, C. 1988. The collective strategy framework: An application to competing predictions of isomorphism. *Administrative Science Quarterly*, 33: 543–61.

Padgett, J.F. and Ansell, C.K. 1993. Robust action and the rise of the Medici, 1400–1434. *American Journal of Sociology*, 98: 1259–319.

Pettigrew, A.M. 1972. Information control as a power resource, *Sociology*, 6: 187–204.

Pfeffer, J. 1983. Organizational demography. *Research in Organizational Behavior*, 5: 299–357.

Pfeffer, J. 1993. Barriers to the advance of organizational science: Paradigm development as a dependent variable. *Academy of Management Review*, 18: 599–620.

Pfeffer, J. and Salancik, G.R. 1978. *The external control of organizations*. New York: Harper & Row.

Podolny, J.M. 1993. A status-based model of market competition. *American Journal of Sociology*, 98: 829–72.

Podolny, J.M. 1998. Network forms of organization. *Annual Review of Sociology*, 24: 57–76.

Podolny, J.M. and Baron, J.N. 1997. Resources and relationships: Social networks and mobility in the workplace. *American Sociological Review*, 62: 673–93.

Podolny, J.M., Stuart, T.E. and Hannan, M.T. 1996. Networks, knowledge, and niches: Competition in the worldwide semiconductor industry, 1984–1991. *American Journal of Sociology*, 102: 659–89.

Polzer, J.T., Milton, L.P. and Swann, W.B. 2002. Capitalizing on diversity: Interpersonal congruence in small work groups. *Administrative Science Quarterly*, 47: 296–324.

Portes, A. 2000. The two meanings of social capital. *Sociological Forum*, 15: 1–12.

Powell, W.W. 1990. Neither market nor hierarchy: Network forms of organization. *Research in Organizational Behavior*, 12: 295–336.

Powell, W.W., Koput, K.W. and Smith-Doerr, L. 1996. Interorganizational collaboration and the locus of innovation: Networks of learning in biotechnology. *Administrative Science Quarterly*, 41: 116–45.

Powell, W.W. and Smith-Doerr, L. 1994. Networks and economic life. In N.J. Smelser and R. Swedberg (eds), *The handbook of economic sociology*, pp. 368–402. Princeton, NJ: Princeton University Press.

Provan, K.G. and Sebastian, J.G. 1998. Networks within networks: Service link overlap, organizational cliques, and network effectiveness. *Academy of Management Journal*, 41: 453–63.

Putnam, R.D. 1993. *Making democracy work*. Princeton, NJ: Princeton University Press.

Putnam, R.D. 1996. The strange disappearance of civic America. *American Prospect*, 24: 34–48.

Raider, H. and Krackhardt, D. 2002. Intraorganizational networks. In J.A.C. Baum (ed.), *The Blackwell companion to organizations*, pp. 58–74. Oxford: Blackwell.

Reed, M.I. 1997. In praise of duality and dualism: Rethinking agency and structure in organizational analysis. *Organization Studies*, 18: 21–42.

Riley, D. and Eckenrode, J. 1986. Social ties: Subgroup differences in costs and benefits. *Journal of Personality and Social Psychology*, 51: 770–8.

Roethlisberger, F.J. and Dickson, W.J. 1939. *Management and the worker.* Cambridge, MA: Harvard University Press.

Rook, K.S. 1984. The negative side of social interaction: Impact on psychological well-being. *Journal of Personality and Social Psychology*, 46: 1097–108.

Rorty, R. 1979. *Philosophy and the mirror of nature.* Princeton, NJ: Princeton University Press.

Salancik, G.R. 1995. Wanted: A good network theory of organization. *Administrative Science Quarterly*, 40: 345–9.

Sampson, E.E. and Insko, C.A. 1964. Cognitive consistency and conformity in the autokinetic situation. *Journal of Abnormal and Social Psychology*, 68: 184–92.

Sampson, S.F. 1968. A novitiate in a period of change: An experimental and case study of relationships. Unpublished PhD dissertation, Sociology Department, Cornell University.

Saxenian, A. 1990. Regional networks and the resurgence of Silicon Valley. *California Management Review*, 33 (1): 89–112.

Saxenian, A. 1994. *Regional advantage: Culture and competition in Silicon Valley and Route 128.* Cambridge, MA: Harvard University Press.

Schensul, J.J, LeCompte, M.D., Trotter, R.T., Cromley, E.K. and Singer, M. 1999. *Mapping social networks, spatial data, and hidden populations.* Walnut Creek, CA: Altamira Press.

Scott, J. 2000. *Social network analysis: A handbook.* 2nd edn. Newbury Park, CA: Sage.

Seeman, T.E., Kaplan, G.A, Knudsen, L., Cohen, R. and Guralnik, J. 1987. Social ties and mortality in the elderly: A comparative analysis of age-dependent patterns of association. *American Journal of Epidemiology*, 126: 714–23.

Seidel, M.-D.L., Polzer, J.T. and Stewart, K.J. 2000. Friends in high places: The effects of social networks on discrimination in salary negotiations. *Administrative Science Quarterly*, 45: 1–24.

Sherif, M. 1936. *The psychology of social norms.* New York: Harper.

Shrader, C.B., Lincoln, J.R. and Hoffman, A.N. 1989. The network structures of organizations: Effects of task contingencies and distributional form. *Human Relations*, 42: 43–66.

Simmel, G. 1908/1950. *The sociology of Georg Simmel.* Glencoe, IL: Free Press.

Simmel, G. 1955. *Conflict: The web of group-affiliations.* Glencoe, IL: Free Press.

Simmel, G. 1971. *Georg Simmel on individuality and social forms.* Edited by D.N. Levine Chicago: University of Chicago Press.

Smith, A. 1979. *The wealth of nations.* Edited by Andrew Skinner. Baltimore, MD: Penguin.

Snyder, M. 1974. Self-monitoring of expressive behavior. *Journal of Personality and Social Psychology*, 30: 526–37.

Snyder, M. 1979. Self-monitoring processes. *Advances in Experimental Social Psychology*, 12: 85–128.

Snyder, M. 1987. *Public appearances/private realities: The psychology of self-monitoring.* New York: Freeman.

Snyder, M. and Gangestad, S. 1982. Choosing social situations: Two investigations of self-monitoring processes. *Journal of Personality and Social Psychology*, 43: 123–35.

Snyder, M. and Gangestad, S. 1986. On the nature of self-monitoring: Matters of assessment, matters of validity. *Journal of Personality and Social Psychology*, 51: 125–39.

Snyder, M., Gangestad, S. and Simpson, J.A. 1983. Choosing friends as activity partners: The role of self-monitoring. *Journal of Personality and Social Psychology*, 51: 181–90.

Stauth, G. and Turner, B.S. 1988. *Nietzsche's dance.* Oxford: Blackwell.

Strang, D. and Tuma, N.B. 1993. Spatial and temporal heterogeneity in diffusion. *American Sociological Review*, 99: 614–39.

Taborsky, E. 1997. *The textual society.* Toronto: Toronto University Press.

Taylor, S.E. 1981. A categorization approach to stereotyping. In D.L. Hamilton (ed.), *Cognitive processes in stereotyping and intergroup behavior*, pp. 83–114. Hillsdale, NJ: Erlbaum.

Taylor, S.E. and Fiske, S.T. 1978. Salience, attention, and attribution: Top of the head phenomena. *Advances in Experimental Social Psychology*, 11: 249–88.

Thomas, W.I. 1927. Social personality: Organization of attitudes. In W.I. Thomas and F. Znaniecki, *The polish peasant in Europe and America*, vol. II, pp. 1831–63. New York: Knopf.

Thomas, W.I. 1966. *On social organization and social personality.* Chicago: University of Chicago Press.

Thompson, J.D. 1967. *Organizations in action.* New York: McGraw-Hill.

Thompson, P. 1993. Postmodernism: Fatal distraction. In J. Hassard and M. Parker (eds), *Postmodernism and organizations*, pp. 183–203. London: Sage.

Tichy, N. 1973. An analysis of clique formation and structure in organizations. *Administrative Science Quarterly*, 18: 194–208.

Tilly, C. 2001. Welcome to the seventeenth century. In P. DiMaggio (ed.), *The twenty-first-century firm*, pp. 200–9. Princeton, NJ: Princeton University Press.

Travers, J. and Milgram, S. 1969. An experimental study of the small world problem. *Sociometry*, 32: 425–43.

Tsai, W. 2000. Social capital, strategic relatedness, and the formation of intra-organizational linkages. *Strategic Management Journal*, 21: 925–39.

Tsai, W. 2001. Knowledge transfer in intra-organizational networks: Effects of network position and absorptive capacity on business unit innovation and performance. *Academy of Management Journal*, 44: 996–1004.

Tsai, W. 2002. Social structure of 'coopetition' within a multiunit organization: Coordination, competition, and intraorganizational knowledge sharing. *Organization Science*, 13: 179–90.

Tsai, W. and Ghoshal, S. 1998. Social capital and value creation: The role of intra-firm networks. *Academy of Management Journal*, 41: 464–76.

Tsai, W. and Kilduff, M. 2002. A structural approach to knowledge transfer: Cross-block ties and business unit performance. Working paper, Smeal College of Business Administration, Pennsylvania State University.

Turkle, S. 1984. *The second self: Computers and the human spirit.* New York: Simon & Schuster.

Tushman, M.L. and Romanelli, E. 1985. Organizational evolution: A metamorphosis model of convergence and reorientation. *Research in Organizational Behavior,* 77: 171–222.

Tutzauer, F. 1985. Toward a theory of disintegration in communication networks. *Social Networks,* 7: 263–85.

Uzzi, B. 1996. The sources and consequences of embeddedness for the economic performance of organizations: The network effect. *American Sociological Review,* 61: 674–98.

Van de Ven, A.H. and Poole, M.S. 1995. Explaining development and change in organizations. *Academy of Management Review,* 20: 510–40.

Van den Bulte, C. and Lilien, G.L. 2001. Medical innovation revisited: Social contagion versus marketing effort. *American Journal of Sociology,* 106: 1409–35.

Van Maanen, J. 1988. *Tales of the field: On writing ethnography.* Chicago: University of Chicago Press.

Van Maanen, J. 1995. Style as theory. *Organization Science,* 6: 133–43.

Walker, G. 1985. Network position and cognition in a computer software firm. *Administrative Science Quarterly,* 30: 103–30.

Warner, W.L. and Lunt, P.S. 1941. *The social life of a modern community.* New Haven, CT: Yale University Press.

Wasserman, S. and Faust, K. 1994. *Social network analysis: Methods and application.* New York: Cambridge University Press.

Wasserman, S. and Iacobucci, D. 1986. Statistical analysis of discrete relational data. *British Journal of Mathematical and Statistical Psychology,* 39: 41–64.

Weick, K.E. 1983. Contradictions in a community of scholars: The cohesion–accuracy tradeoff. *Review of Higher Education,* 6: 253–67.

Weick, K.E. and Bougon, M.G. 1986. Organizations as cognitive maps. In H.P. Sims and D.A. Gioia (eds), *The thinking organization,* pp. 102–35. San Francisco: Jossey-Bass.

Weimann, G. 1982. On the importance of marginality: One more step into the two-step flow of communication. *American Sociological Review,* 47: 764–73.

Weiss, R.S. and Jacobson, E. 1955. A method for the analysis of the structure of complex organizations. *American Sociological Review,* 20: 661–8.

Wellman, B. 1988a. Thinking structurally. In B. Wellman and S.D. Berkowitz (eds), *Social structures: A network approach,* pp. 15–18. Cambridge: Cambridge University Press.

Wellman, B. 1988b. Structural analysis: From method and metaphor to theory and substance. In B. Wellman and S.D. Berkowitz (eds), *Social structures: A network approach,* pp. 19–61. Cambridge: Cambridge University Press.

Wellman, B. and Berkowitz, S.D. 1988. Introduction: Studying social structures. In B. Wellman and S.D. Berkowitz (eds), *Social structures: A network approach,* pp. 1–14. Cambridge: Cambridge University Press.

White, H.C. 1961. Management conflict and sociometric structure. *American Journal of Sociology*, 67: 185–99.

White, H.C. 1970. *Chains of opportunity: System models of mobility in organizations.* Cambridge, MA: Harvard University Press.

White, H.C. 1992. *Identity and control: A structural theory of social action.* Princeton, NJ: Princeton University Press.

White, H.C., Boorman, S.A. and Breiger, R.L. 1976. Social structures from multiple networks: Blockmodels of roles and positions. *American Journal of Sociology*, 81: 730–79.

Yager, J. 2002. *When friendship hurts: How to deal with friends who betray, abandon, or wound you.* New York: Simon & Shuster.

Zaccaro, S.J., Foti, R.J. and Kenny, D.A. 1991. Self-monitoring and trait-based variance in leadership: An investigation of leader flexibility across multiple group situations. *Journal of Applied Psychology*, 76: 308–15.

Zachary, W.W. 1977. An information flow model for conflict and fission in small groups. *Journal of Anthropological Research*, 33: 452–73.

Zeggelink, E. 1995. Evolving friendship networks: An individual-oriented approach implementing similarity. *Social Networks*, 17: 83–110.

Name Index

Subject Index